CONTENTS

FOREWARD

FOREWARD

As a boy I used to hear people talk about walking in the footsteps of Jesus. Then as a teenager I heard Pastor Eva Devon preach on "In His Steps" and how we should walk in the footsteps of God. I saw the movie based on Charles Monroe Sheldon's book, "In His Steps". Others also said that we should walk in God's footsteps.

Later on in life I read the Footsteps poem by Margaret Fishback Powers and was impressed. However, none of the people I heard ever said where the footsteps of God lead or what they were like. I began to study about where God walked and what it meant to mankind. I discovered that some of God's steps are for Him to walk alone and do not follow a path that we are to walk in. Other steps of God are the steps that we can and ought to walk in as well.

I hope this helps to define our walk with God a little bit better and draws each one closer in relationship with the God who desires to walk with us.

Chapter One   Footsteps of Fellowship

The background for the first set of footsteps we find in the Bible is found in Genesis 1:25-31: **And God made the beast of the earth according to its kind, cattle according to its kind, and everything that creeps on the earth according to its kind. And God saw that it was good. Then God said, "Let Us make man in Our image, according to Our likeness; let them have dominion over the fish of the sea, over the birds of the air, and over the cattle, over all the earth and over every creeping thing that creeps on the earth." So God created man in His own image; in the image of God He created him; male and female He created them. Then God blessed them, and God said to them, "Be fruitful and multiply; fill the earth and subdue it; have dominion over the fish of the sea, over the birds of the air, and over every living thing that moves on the earth."And God said, "See, I have given you every herb that yields seed which is on the face of all the earth, and every tree whose fruit yields** seed; to you it shall be for food. Also, to every beast of the earth, to every bird of the air, and to everything that creeps on the earth, in which there is life, I have given every green herb for food"; and it was so. Then God saw everything that He had made, and indeed it was very good. So the evening and the morning were the sixth day. This is the picture of creation of mankind on the earth. Until this time there was no-one on earth to follow in God's footsteps or to walk with Him.

Once man had been created, we find that God comes to the garden where He had placed the man and woman that He had created in order to walk with them. In fact, God created mankind so that He would have someone with whom to fellowship. After Adam and Eve, the man and woman, had sinned we read in Genesis 3:8, **And they heard the sound of the LORD God walking in the garden in the cool of the day, and Adam and his wife hid themselves from the presence of the LORD God among the trees of the garden.** Obviously God had walked in the garden often in order to walk with Adam and Eve for fellowship. This is amazing. The creator wanting to fellowship with the creation. Notice that the first question God ever asked mankind is found in Genesis 3:9: **Then the LORD God called to Adam and said to him, "Where *are* you?"** The Lord God was looking for man for fellowship.

Lets look at the subject of fellowship. Fellowship is an old English word that comes from two fellows in a ship travelling the same direction together. The dictionary meaning is "companionship, association...having common interests, ideals, experiences, etc." It holds the idea of brotherhood or family.

God wants fellowship with His human creation. God created all mankind for His own glory - Isaiah 43:7 is God speaking: **Everyone who is called by My name, whom I have created for My glory; I have formed him, yes, I have made him."** This tells us much about mankind and God. Mankind is a reflection of God Himself. In Genesis 1:26 & 27 we read, **Then God said, "Let Us make man in Our image, according to Our likeness; let them have dominion over the fish of the sea, over the birds of the** air, and over the cattle, over all the earth and over every creeping thing that creeps on the earth." So God created man in His own image; in the image of God He created him; male and female He created them. Obviously this was not a physical image for "God is Spirit, and those who worship Him must worship in spirit and truth." (John 4:24) God created us in the physical sense as his sons and daughters of creation. The apostle Paul said of God in Acts 17:28 & 29, "for in Him we live and move and have our being, as also some of your own poets have said, `For we are also His offspring.' Therefore, since we are the offspring of God, we ought not to think that the Divine Nature is like gold or silver or stone, something shaped by art and man's devising." As God's physical creation, mankind is an extension of God to the rest of the world

Having the image of God means that we are owned by Him. We hear Jesus saying in Matt 22:20 & 21, ..."Whose image and inscription is this?" They said to Him, "Caesar's." And He said to them, "Render therefore to

Caesar the things that are Caesar's, and to God the things that are God's." If you bear the image of Caesar, you are Caesar's but since we bear the image of God, regardless of how marred it has become by sin, we are God's possession.

As we look more into God's footsteps of fellowship we find God's footsteps first of all in the Garden of Eden. Remember the words of Genesis 3:8: **And they heard the sound of the LORD God walking in the garden in the cool of the day, and Adam and his wife hid themselves**. God's purpose in walking in the garden, that we know as the Garden of Eden, was to talk with His human creation. God wanted fellowship with man. God created mankind for fellowship and He has always wanted His creation to walk with Him. It is evident from the first three chapters of the book of Genesis that God often walked with man, talking with him in the garden. Nowhere in Scripture do we find that God chose to walk with any of the rest of His creation in order to have fellowship with Him.

We need to understand the nature of God's fellowship with mankind. We can relate it to human fellowship on this earth. There are some similarities.

Fellowship is based on the relationship between persons. If men are antique car buffs you will hear fellowship centering around the subject of old cars. If women are into cooking or crafts, their fellowship will be around cooking or crafts. We have already seen that the relationship between God and mankind was that of mankind being God's physical offspring. In the physical sense we are the sons and daughters of God by creation of God. God created mankind to be His physical family. Therefore, this fellowship is a family fellowship with God being our heavenly Father. The created earth with all aspects of this creation was to be a family operation with man being part of it. The relationship of God and mankind was in regards to the creation of the earth. Genesis 1:26 reveals this: **Then God said, "Let Us make man in Our image, according to Our likeness; let them have dominion over the fish of the sea, over the birds of the air, and over the cattle,**

over all the earth and over every creeping thing that creeps on the earth." Andrew Murray in his book, "With Christ in the School of Prayer", wrote, "Man's destiny appears clearly from God's language at creation. It was to *fill, to subdue, to have dominion* over the earth and all in it. All the three expressions show us that man was meant, as God's representative, to hold rule here on earth. As God's viceroy he was to fill God's place: himself subject to God, he was to keep all else in subjection to Him. It was the will of God that all that was to be done on earth should be done through him: the history of the earth was to be entirely in his hands." We see a family business here with fellowship revolving around the operation of earthly things according to God's will.

This fellowship was that of a servant or steward for the benefit of the Father and the good of creation. Genesis 1:28 states, **Then God blessed them, and God said to them, "Be fruitful and multiply; fill the earth and subdue it; have dominion over the fish of the sea, over the birds of the air, and over every living thing that moves on the** earth." We read in Genesis 2:15-17, **Then the LORD God took the man and put him in the garden of Eden to tend and keep it. And the LORD God commanded the man, saying, "Of every tree of the garden you may freely eat; but of the tree of the knowledge of good and evil you shall not eat, for in the day that you eat of it you shall surely die."** As servants of God, mankind was to tend the garden and to take dominion over the whole of creation on the basis of being the offspring of God with a commission to serve as servants.

Only one negative command was given to Adam and Eve and that was to not eat from the tree of the knowledge of good and evil . This tree did not appear to be a special tree in any way. It had fruit, although we have no idea what the fruit was: Some have suggested an apple, some a pomegranate, some say figs and another suggested, tongue in cheek, a lemon, because it soured all humanity. The fruit had no special power in itself. Eating something forbidden would cause them to know what evil was for the first time by their experience and show them the difference between what they initially had been and what they had then become.

By walking in obedience to God, mankind had the privilege of walking in fellowship with Him. By disobeying God there were disastrous results. Broken fellowship resulted. The Bible is clear as to what happened. The snake or serpent, that Revelation 12:9 identifies as the Devil and Satan, tricked Eve into eating the forbidden fruit and Adam agreed to follow Eve's example. Immediately spiritual death came to mankind and physical death would follow later on. The warning by God in the Hebrew in Genesis 2: 16 & 17 holds the idea of "**In the day that you eat of it dying you shall die**". Disobedience to God or sin, as it is called, broke fellowship with God.

First of all, mankind realized their nakedness before God and hid from God. Genesis 3:8 tells us, **And they heard the sound of the LORD God walking in the garden in the cool of the day, and Adam and his wife hid themselves from the presence of the LORD God among the trees of the garden.** God had to judge the sin of mankind. The serpent was judged for his evil part. The woman was judged for her part. The man was judged for his part. We read this in Genesis 3:14-19: **So the LORD God said to the serpent: " Because you have done this, You *are* cursed more than all cattle, And more than every beast of the field; On your belly you shall go, And you shall eat dust All the days of your life. And I will put enmity Between you and the woman, And between your seed and her Seed; He shall bruise your head, And you shall bruise His heel." To the woman He said: " I will greatly multiply your sorrow and your conception; In pain you shall bring forth children; Your desire *shall be* for your husband, And he shall rule over you." Then to Adam He said, "Because you have heeded the voice of your wife, and have eaten from the tree of which I commanded you, saying, 'You shall not eat of it': " Cursed *is* the ground for your sake; In toil you shall eat *of* it All the days of your life. Both thorns and thistles it shall bring forth for you, And you shall eat the herb of the field. In the sweat of your face you shall eat bread Till you** return to the ground, For out of it you were taken; For dust you *are,* And to dust you shall return." Genesis 2:24 says that God then had them chased out of the garden to live on the earth without the bountiful blessing of God on them. One little boy heard his Sunday School teacher say that God drove Adam and Eve out of the garden of Eden and he thought that it was amazing that God had a car to drive way back then. The teacher explained that driving the man and woman from the garden meant that He forced them out by chasing them.

Sin separated mankind from the footsteps of fellowship with God. Isaiah 59:2 describes it well: **But your iniquities have separated you from your God; and your sins have hidden His face from you, so that He will not hear.** Sin cuts us off from fellowship with God. All mankind falls under the curse of sin because we have all sinned: Romans 5:12 shows this: **Therefore, just as through one man sin entered the world, and death through sin, and thus death spread to all men, because all sinned--** This not only means that all people sin but that all have sinned in the person of Adam who passed on his wretched corruption to the rest of us. Romans 3:10 puts it this way: **As it is written: "There is none righteous, no, not one;** Romans 5:19 elaborates on this comparing what Adam did to us with what Jesus did for us: **For as by one man's disobedience many were made sinners, so by the obedience of one shall many be made righteous**.

Fellowship was made possible between God and mankind by God Himself. Only God could initiate a return to fellowship because our sins had cut mankind off from God. In the garden of Eden God created the first animal sacrifice by killing at least one animal and making a skin covering for Adam and Eve. Genesis 3:21 shares this: **Also for Adam and his wife the LORD God made tunics of skin, and clothed them.** The blood of at least one animal was shed to cover their nakedness and sinfulness: the innocent for the guilty.

Without blood being shed God cannot forgive sins. God is holy and just so that He cannot let sin go unpunished. Hebrews 9:22b tells us, **without shedding of blood there**

is no remission (forgiveness).

God set up a system of sacrifices in order to renew fellowship with mankind by covering their sins temporarily. Hebrews 10:1-3 declares, **For the law, having a shadow of the good things to come, and not the very image of the things, can never with these same sacrifices, which they offer continually year by year, make those who approach perfect. For then would they not have ceased to be offered? For the worshipers, once purified, would have had no more consciousness of sins. But in those sacrifices there is a reminder of sins every year.** Hebrews 10:11 shows the weakness of this system of sacrifices: **And every priest stands ministering daily and offering repeatedly the same sacrifices, which can never take away sins.** The sacrifices could only cover over the sins of the people for a year and then had to be repeated again every year afterwards.

However, God had a plan which He enacted so that sins could be removed and fellowship could be restored by one final sacrifice.

In due time God sent His own Son, Jesus Christ, to give His life on the cross for the sins of all mankind: 1 John 3:5 tells us, **And you know that He was manifested to take away our sins, and in Him there is no sin.**

Although God initiated a way back to renewed fellowship we also have a part in renewing fellowship with God. Those who receive the sacrifice of Jesus Christ as theirs and choose to follow Him have the fellowship of being His offspring renewed in their lives.   John 1:12 joyfully announces, **But as many as received Him, to them He gave the right to become children of God, to those who believe in His name:** In John 6:37 Jesus said, **All that the Father gives Me will come to Me, and the one who comes to Me I will by no means cast out.** 1 Corinthians 1:9 puts it this way: **God is faithful, by whom you were called into the fellowship of His Son, Jesus Christ our Lord**. God is faithful and reaches out to all who will come to Him.

Have you reached out to Him in order to have fellowship with Him? He waits with open arms to receive you. Jesus said in John 6:37, **All that the Father gives Me will come to Me, and the one who comes to Me I will by no means cast out.**

Our fellowship with God means our fellowship with the rest of the body of Christ, the church. I John 1:3 says, **that which we have seen and heard we declare to you, that you also may have fellowship with us; and truly our fellowship is with the Father and with His Son Jesus Christ.**

From this it is evident that our fellowship with the Father and with His Son Jesus Christ means that we will have fellowship with the body of Christ, the church. Those who say that God has pulled them away from other believers to serve God on their own are acting contrary to God's Word and need to repent and renew fellowship with the other believers.

Walking with God in the footsteps of fellowship is something that we do continually. I John 1:6 & 7 puts it this way, **If we say that we have fellowship with Him, and walk in darkness, we lie and do not practice the truth.**

But if we walk in the light as He is in the light, we have fellowship with one another, and the blood of Jesus Christ His Son cleanses us from all sin. This means walking continually with God and His body, the church, in fellowship.

God has prepared the way for us to walk with Him in close fellowship. How close we get to God in fellowship depends on how close we walk with Him in obedience and communion. This also means having loving fellowship with the family of God as well.

Let us start to walk on the pathway to fellowship with God by receiving Jesus as our Saviour and then walk as close as we can to the Lord and His church in the footsteps of fellowship.

Chapter Two   Footsteps of Forgiveness

Forgiveness was necessary in order to renew the fellowship with God that once mankind had in the Garden of Eden. When Adam and Eve ate of the forbidden fruit, all of creation was affected. Romans 8:22 declares, **For we know that the whole creation groans and labors with birth pangs together until now.** Human relationship with God was spiritually cut off. Mankind needed forgiveness.

The footsteps of forgiveness are essential if we are to have any kind of relationship with God, our creator. The dilemma was clear. Ezekiel 18:4 explains the problem, **" Behold, all souls are Mine; The soul of the father As well as the soul of the son is Mine; The soul who sins shall die."** Death came to mankind, both physical and spiritual, when Adam and Eve chose to disobey God and introduce sin into the world.

A life had to be taken as a judgment on sin. We all deserve to die because of our sinfulness because as it says in Romans 3:23, **for all have sinned and fall short of the**

glory of God.

Blood had to be shed in order to have sins covered and then later on, removed. Hebrews 9:22 makes it clear: **And according to the law almost all things are purified with blood, and without shedding of blood there is no remission** (forgiveness). The reason that blood had to be shed is because blood is the carrier of life in the body. Leviticus 17:11 says, **For the life of the flesh *is* in the blood, and I have given it to you upon the altar to make atonement for your souls; for it *is* the blood *that* makes atonement for the soul.'** In other words, since the life of the body is in the blood, when the blood is poured out it is the source of life leaving the body. There can be no doubt about it; the body that has lost its blood, short of an amazing miracle, is dead.

The blood was proof that a body had died for sins when it was offered as a sacrifice to God. This was done yearly by the high priest in Israel. Hebrews 9:6-10 explains: **Now when these things had been thus prepared, the priests always went into the first part of the tabernacle,** performing the services. But into the second part the high priest *went* alone once a year, not without blood, which he offered for himself and *for* the people's sins *committed* in ignorance; the Holy Spirit indicating this, that the way into the Holiest of All was not yet made manifest while the first tabernacle was still standing. It *was* symbolic for the present time in which both gifts and sacrifices are offered which cannot make him who performed the service perfect in regard to the conscience --- *concerned* only with foods and drinks, various washings, and fleshly ordinances imposed until the time of reformation. This could not remove sins but only cover them for a year. A better sacrifice of blood had to be given.

What was needed was the shed blood of a man for the sins of mankind but any man on earth who would die was sinful and could only die for his own sins. Only an innocent sinless person could die and have his sins shed to pay for the sins of sinful mankind. Since only God was without sin, only God could perform this function. However,

God is eternal and cannot die so this was an obstacle to our forgiveness.

The path to our forgiveness was fulfilled when God overshadowed a young virgin, Mary, and put His life into her womb creating a sinless, sanctified baby. Romans 5:19 speaking of Adam says, **...by one man's disobedience many were made sinners...** Mankind on earth was corrupted by a sinful nature from Adam's sin but this baby, born of a virgin, was not contaminated by the sinful nature passed on to all mankind by the man. This was the God-man, Jesus Christ our Lord.

The cost for our forgiveness was the shed blood of Jesus Christ as He took our sins and iniquities on Himself, paying the full price for all sin for all mankind once and for all. Hebrews 10:12-14 declares, **But this Man, after He had offered one sacrifice for sins forever, sat down at the right hand of God, from that time waiting till His enemies are made His footstool. For by one offering He has perfected forever those who are being sanctified.** Hebrews 9:11-14 puts it this way: **But Christ came *as* High**

Priest of the good things to come, with the greater and more perfect tabernacle not made with hands, that is, not of this creation. Not with the blood of goats and calves, but with His own blood He entered the Most Holy Place once for all, having obtained eternal redemption. For if the blood of bulls and goats and the ashes of a heifer, sprinkling the unclean, sanctifies for the purifying of the flesh, how much more shall the blood of Christ, who through the eternal Spirit offered Himself without spot to God, cleanse your conscience from dead works to serve the living God?

God always initiates the footsteps that we are to follow in. God loves first and then His love in us gives us the ability to love. 1 John 4:19 makes this clear: **We love Him because He first loved us.** God also walks in forgiveness towards us so that we can walk in forgiveness towards others.

That God walks in forgiveness is seen in one of Jesus' parables. Luke 15:11-24 is the story of a rebellious young man. The story begins like this (verses 11-16): **A** certain man had two sons. And the younger of them said to his father, "Father, give me the portion of goods that falls to me." So he divided to them his livelihood. And not many days after, the younger son gathered all together, journeyed to a far country, and there wasted his possessions with prodigal (wasteful) living. But when he had spent all, there arose a severe famine in that land, and he began to be in want. Then he went and joined himself to a citizen of that country, and he sent him into his fields to feed swine. And he would gladly have filled his stomach with the pods that the swine ate, and no one gave him anything.

Let's put the story in its actual setting. Here is a Jewish family, obviously of means, doing quite well in life with a big farm, servants and so on. The youngest of two sons decides he has had enough and wants his inheritance so he can go and explore the world. First of all, it was not his right to demand his inheritance. In Israel, the inheritance was to be given out after the father died or at the father's request just when he knew he would soon pass away. The eldest son would get a double portion of inheritance and the father's family blessing and then he would be responsible to divide the rest of the inheritance with his siblings unless the father was still alive and chose to do it himself.

When the father divided the inheritance between his two sons, the eldest would get the double portion and the youngest would get what was left and that is all he would ever get from his dad. But this fellow demanded his inheritance while his father was still well and healthy. Note that the father recognized the young man's request and allowed him to act according to his selfish desires. He divided the inheritance and gave the young man his portion. The young man headed for a distant country to see the world, as many young people do today. Then this young man wasted his money and goods on wild living. He had money to spend and he found that there were many who were willing to help him spend it. He ended up destitute with nothing, not even something to eat. He finally joined himself to a citizen of the foreign country (not hired by him) and was sent to feed his pigs (for a Jewish man to feed pigs was unthinkable as the pig was an unclean animal). Note that he was not paid a salary, otherwise he could have bought food. He was ready to eat the bean pods that he was feeding the pigs because he had nothing else.

The steps of forgiveness are seen as the story continues in verses 17-24. The young man eventually "came to himself" - obviously he was not with himself - he was not in his right mind or thinking up to this point. (Anyone who forsakes the love and care of the heavenly Father is not thinking right either.) He recognized that his father's servants had more to eat than he did while he was facing starvation. He decided to go back home and confess his wrongdoing against both heaven and his father and become a hired servant instead of a son. This is the first time we see humility and regret in this young man. He headed back home. The father saw him coming a long distance away and he ran to meet his son; these were the steps of forgiveness. The young man made a confession of wrongdoing but before he could ask to become a hired servant, the father got his servants to put the best robe they could find on him and a ring on his hand (possibly a family ring signifying acceptance back into the family) and sandals on his feet. Then the father called for a big party to celebrate the young man's return. This is the story of forgiveness.

However, the story does not end at this point. The eldest brother was working in the fields and he asked a servant what the commotion was all about. The servant said what had happened but the eldest brother got angry. No rejoicing with this man! The father came to the eldest son to get him to come to the party but the eldest son, in self-pity, said that it wasn't fair because he had served faithfully all these years and had not as much as a young goat given for a party with his friends but his sinful bother was getting the royal treatment. The father's answer is significant: **Son, you are always with me, and all that I have is yours. It was right that we should make merry and be glad, for your brother was dead and is alive again, and was lost and is found.** Forgiveness first came from the dad and then was expected in the eldest son as well. The eldest son had forgotten that all of the inheritance that was left was his. His younger brother had blown all the money that he had inherited so he had to make a living starting from scratch without his dad's help. The real issue was that his brother had returned with a repentant heart and needed to be forgiven.

This parable teaches us a lot about God's forgiveness as it is a picture of His footsteps toward rebellious mankind. God does not stop people from claiming what is legally not theirs to claim nor does He stop people from rebelling against Him (it is called free will). God is always watching for those who would repent and return to Him in humility. God runs with forgiveness to us when we repent and return to Him.

The dad in this parable is a representation of God but God is always greater, more loving, purer and more gracious than our earthly fathers for He is our kind and perfect heavenly Father. If your earthly father is a bad father, remember that God also waits with love for him to repent and come to Him for forgiveness. Since we have all done wrong, we need to come to God humbly, ask for forgiveness and accept Jesus Christ as our sacrifice for sins and follow Him

One clear lesson is that God expects us to forgive even as He forgives. He walks in forgiveness and He expects us to walk in forgiveness as well. O course, God walks in steps of forgiveness before we can. In other words, we cannot properly forgive until we have received God's forgiveness. As we have noted in chapter one, God initiated forgiveness right after Adam and Eve sinned for the first time. Genesis 3:21 says, **Also for Adam and his wife the LORD God made tunics of skin, and clothed them.** According to Genesis 2:25 they were unclothed, living together as husband and wife. Their sin revealed their nakedness to them so God made the first sacrifice for sin by killing and animal and making tunics of skin to cover their nakedness. God Himself initiated the path of forgiveness back to Himself by animal sacrifice. God's forgiveness comes through His loving grace (favour). Ephesians 1:7 says, **In Him** (Jesus Christ) **we have redemption through**

His blood, the forgiveness of sins, according to the riches of His grace. Grace means favour and with God's grace it means favour from God that one does not deserve.

God's forgiveness brings the fear of God. Psalm 130:4 says, **But there is forgiveness with You (God), That You may be feared.** Forgiveness opens us to the awesome greatness of who God is. We need to walk in the fear of God, not terrorized by God, but rather, cautiously endeavouring to be pleasing to Him whom we love for His great love toward us with great awe and respect. Psalm 25:14 assures us, **The secret of the LORD is with those who fear Him, And He will show them His covenant.**

God's forgiveness comes through the Lord Jesus. Acts 5:30 & 31 are the words of the apostle Peter, **The God of our fathers raised up Jesus whom you murdered by hanging on a tree. Him God has exalted to His right hand to be Prince and Savior, to give repentance to Israel and forgiveness of sins.** Also, Colossians 1:14 says of Jesus, **in whom we have redemption through His blood, the forgiveness of sins.**

God's forgiveness brings justification. Justification means that we are declared just or not guilty. Acts 13:38 & 39 speaks of Jesus: **Therefore let it be known to you, brethren, that through this Man is preached to you the forgiveness of sins; and by Him everyone who believes is justified from all things from which you could not be justified by the law of Moses.** The forgiveness of God means that you are no longer guilty and have no condemnation against you when you turn your life over to Christ Jesus. God's forgiveness brings the Gentiles into the family of God and makes the Jews and Gentiles one in Jesus Christ.

God told the apostle Paul in Acts 26:17 & 18, **I will deliver you from the Jewish people, as well as from the Gentiles, to whom I now send you, to open their eyes, in order to turn them from darkness to light, and from the power of Satan to God, that they may receive forgiveness of sins and an inheritance among those who are sanctified by faith in Me.** All mankind can be assured of salvation and an eternal inheritance with the family of God because of the forgiveness of God made available to all.

Having received forgiveness from God we are to walk in the same forgiveness towards others. It is evident from the parable of the prodigal son that the father forgave and expected His son to forgive also - of course, this is a picture of our loving heavenly Father who forgives freely and wishes us to forgive as well. We read in Matthew 18:21 & 22, **Then Peter came to Him** (Jesus) **and said, "Lord, how often shall my brother sin against me, and I forgive him? Up to seven times?" Jesus said to him, "I do not say to you, up to seven times, but up to seventy times seven."** Jesus meant seventy times seven in one day because Peter was referring to an earlier conversation in Luke 17:4 where Jesus said, **"If he sins against you seven times in a day , and seven times in a day returns to you, saying, 'I repent,' you shall forgive him."** Peter thought that he had it figured out. He only had to forgive someone seven times in a day and then he could get even. Jesus wanted to correct that error and show that seven

32

times in a day or seventy times seven times in a day meant do not stop forgiving. I calculated how often you would have to forgive someone who sins against you in a day if you obey Jesus to forgive seventy times seven. That would mean that if someone sins against you every three minutes in a day including night time, you would forgive him each time. In other words, just as God does not stop forgiving us no matter how many times we sin against Him, we are to walk in His footsteps and forgive others as well over and over and over again.

Not only are we expected to walk in footsteps of forgiveness but we are commanded to do so at the risk of losing God's forgiveness. Matthew 6:14 & 15 warns us, **For if you forgive men their trespasses, your heavenly Father will also forgive you. But if you do not forgive men their trespasses, neither will your Father forgive your trespasses.** From the parable of the unforgiving servant we read in Matthew 18:34 & 35, **And his master was angry, and delivered him to the torturers until he should pay all that was due him. So My heavenly Father**

also will do to you if each of you, from his heart, does not forgive his brother his trespasses. Again in Mark 11:25 & 26 we read, **And whenever you stand praying, if you have anything against anyone, forgive him, that your Father in heaven may also forgive you your trespasses. But if you do not forgive, neither will your Father forgive your trespasses.**

Matthew 5:23 & 24 also states, **Therefore if you bring your gift to the altar, and there remember that your brother has something against you, leave your gift there before the altar, and go your way. First be reconciled to your brother, and then come and offer your gift.**

Walking in the footsteps of forgiveness is not optional. It is commanded over and over. God expects us to obey because it is the path that He walks.

Walking in forgiveness is opposite to our sinful nature. Matthew 5:44-46 instructs us, **But I say to you, love your enemies, bless those who curse you, do good to those who hate you, and pray for those who**

spitefully use you and persecute you, that you may be sons of your Father in heaven; for He makes His sun rise on the evil and on the good, and sends rain on the just and on the unjust. For if you love those who love you, what reward have you? Do not even the tax collectors do the same? In the natural we want to get even or at least pray fire down on those who sin against us but this is not God's way. Even on the cross we read in Luke 23:34, **Then Jesus said, "Father, forgive them for they do not know what they do."**...

Forgiveness means that you do not require or desire retribution for what has been done to you. 2 Corinthians 2:6 & 7 tells the people in the church to ease off in punishment towards a man who had done wrong: **This punishment which was inflicted by the majority is sufficient for such a man, so that, on the contrary, you ought rather to forgive and comfort him, lest perhaps such a one be swallowed up with too much sorrow.** This man had been punished by the church for his wrongdoing. It is evident that he has now repented of his wrong. Forgiveness is to not require any more punishment and to show him love again.

The footsteps of forgiveness lead to doing good to the one who wronged you. Romans 12:17-21 tells us, **Repay no one evil for evil. Have regard for good things in the sight of all men. If it is possible, as much as depends on you, live peaceably with all men. Beloved, do not avenge yourselves, but rather give place to wrath; for it is written, "Vengeance is Mine, I will repay, " says the Lord. Therefore, "If your enemy is hungry, feed him; If he is thirsty, give him a drink; For in so doing you will heap coals of fire on his head." Do not be overcome by evil, but overcome evil with good.**

Phil Robertson of West Monroe, Louisiana, in his book "Happy, Happy, Happy", chapter 13, pages 189-194, tells an interesting series of events in his life. He read the above portion from Romans and said, "It won't work." Then he thought, "How do I know. I haven't tried it." He was making a living fishing the river. People kept stealing his fish and it was costing him a lot. The next time he saw some men pulling up his nets he jumped in his boat and went out to them. They tried to say they were just fishing but Phil told them bluntly that he knew they were trying to steal his fish. He said, "Evidently, you've planned a fish fry, but y'all aren't catching any. But if you want a fish fry..Well, here's the good news. I'm going to give what you were trying to steal-- free of charge." They started to protest but he emptied his net and filled their boat with fish. Phil told them if they needed fish again not to steal them but come and see him and he would give them some fish. People quit stealing fish and whenever someone did go to his nets he would go out and give them some fish. He gave away less fish than what people had been stealing. Phil reread Romans 12:17-21 and wrote this: "What the Almighty is saying is that no matter how sorry and low-down somebody might be, everybody's worth something. But you're never going to turn them if you're as evil as they are". Since then Phil has had the privilege of leading many to Christ.

You cannot walk in the footsteps of forgiveness by yourself. The pathway is God's pathway. It is the pathway of a godly heart and only God can give you that.

If you feel you cannot forgive, ask God to give you His heart of compassion and a view of His great love for you and the one who hurt you. Then prayerfully place your hand in His and let God lead you in footsteps of forgiveness. It is amazing what God will do!

By the way, after you forgive someone it does not mean that you necessarily trust them. They may continue to do evil towards others. Trust is earned. Forgiveness is a gift. Forgiveness is simply not requiring evil against them in return for what wrong they have done against you.

With the help of the Holy Spirit who lives in us as believers we can forgive. We must forgive. We will joyfully forgive and walk in God's footsteps of forgiveness.

Chapter Three   Footsteps of Friendship

After the footsteps of fellowship with God that we see in the first part of the Bible have been restored through the footsteps of forgiveness, we come upon the footsteps of friendship. Fellowship can take on many forms from a casual relationship to an in-depth relationship. Whereas fellowship is based on common interests, friendship is based on a unity and depth of commitment that simple fellowship does not have. It is a much deeper relationship where trust and understanding take on a new and greater meaning.

We can see this at church gatherings where food is involved. People can fellowship together because of their common interests in Christ and His love. However, some will be special friends with others because of a deeper relationship of love and trust that time has developed.

A look at the Hebrew words from Scripture help to show us the depth of meaning found in God's footsteps of friendship. One word for "friend" is 'âhab 'âhêb*aw-hab', aw-*

habe' which is a primitive root meaning "to *have affection for*". The word for "friendship" is râ'âh*raw-aw'* which is a primitive root for "to *tend* a flock, that is, *pasture* it; intransitively to *graze* (literally or figuratively); generally to *rule*; by extension to *associate* with (as a friend): - companion, keep company with, feed, use as a friend, make friendship with, herdman, keep [sheep] (-er), pastor, shepherd. The definition is quite drawn out but do you get the picture? Please note that friendship is linked to the concept of a pastor or shepherd caring for his sheep. John 10:11-13 reveals the commitment and care a shepherd has for his flock: **I am the good shepherd. The good shepherd gives his life for the sheep. But a hireling, he who is not the shepherd, one who does not own the sheep, sees the wolf coming and leaves the sheep and flees; and the wolf catches the sheep and scatters them. The hireling flees because he is a hireling and does not care about the sheep.** A friend cares for and defends a person as a shepherd does his sheep (a good pastor is the friend of his flock who is committed to them).

The definition of a friend, then, is one for whom a person has affection and it is demonstrated in words and actions. Proverbs17:17 puts it this way, **A friend loves at all times...** The greatest friend is one who is committed to someone regardless of what happens. Proverbs18:24 explains it this way: **A man who has friends must himself be friendly, But there is a friend who sticks closer than a brother.** In fact, a friend loves his or her friend and this commitment is what love is all about. 1 Corinthians 13, often called "The Love Chapter", puts it clearly in verses 4-8: **Love suffers long *and* is kind; love does not envy; love does not parade itself, is not puffed up; does not behave rudely, does not seek its own, is not provoked, thinks no evil; does not rejoice in iniquity, but rejoices in the truth; bears all things, believes all things, hopes all things, endures all things. Love never fails....** Friendship puts up with a lot of things that bring unhappiness or annoyance because that person is a friend. A friend rejoices in the good that comes into a person's life and is not envious of him or her. A friend does not put on airs nor is boastful. A friend will be kind and not rude in any word or action. A friend seeks good for others instead of selfishly looking out for himself. A friend rejoices in the truth and not in wrongdoing. A friend will bear all things in order to be a friend, believing the best, hoping for all good and enduring simply because the love of a friend does not fail. This is definitely the description of God's love for us as a friend of mankind. A gospel song, Whom Shall I Fear", by Chris Tomlin, says, "He is the King of glory. He is a friend of mine; the God of angel armies. He's always by my side." It is true that God wants to be our friend but if we are not walking in His footsteps of friendship, we will not achieve the level of friendship that God has to offer.

A Bible example of God's footsteps of friendship is found in Genesis 5:22-24: **After he begot Methuselah, Enoch walked with God three hundred years, and had sons and daughters. So all the days of Enoch were three hundred and sixty-five years. And Enoch walked with God; and he was not, for God took him.** Enoch walked with God, obviously, very intimately. Consider this, for 300 years Enoch walked in friendship with God. They were so close to each other that they walked together right into eternity. God must have said, "Enough is enough. You are so much like Me through our friendship that you might as well come home with Me forever." Enoch was so close to God in friendship that he walked right into heaven with God, never having faced death as we know it." Obviously Enoch had to have some kind of transformation in his body in order to go to live with God in heaven. Only one other person in Scripture was translated to heaven like Enoch, and that was Elijah (2 Kings 2:1-11).

Abraham also had a close friendship with God. James 2:23 tells us, **And the Scripture was fulfilled which says, "Abraham believed God, and it was accounted to him for righteousness". And he was called the friend of God.** King Jehoshaphat, many hundreds of years after Abraham lived on earth, referred to Abraham as God's friend by reminding God of His great workings on behalf of Israel: In 2 Chronicles 20:7 Jehoshaphat prayed, **Are You not our God, who drove out the inhabitants of this land**

before Your people Israel, and gave it to the descendants of Abraham Your friend forever?

Abraham believed God and showed his friendship with God by walking in the steps of obedience to Canaan even though he did not know where the Lord was leading him. This shows the trust that Abraham had in God. It was the trust of a loyal friend. Others may have said that Abraham was foolhardy, travelling off to who knows where because he believed God told him to do so. When you have a good friend that you know well, you can trust them and when that friend is God, you can absolutely walk with Him in footsteps of friendship with total confidence in the goodness of God and His promises. James 2:23 declares, **And the Scripture was fulfilled which says,** *"Abraham believed God, and it was accounted to him for righteousness."* **And he was called the friend of God.** Abraham's belief in God caused him to act in obedience and this act of faith was credited to him as righteousness before God and it would appear that this was the beginning of a relationship with God that caused him to be called "the friend of God." It is interesting that although Abraham was called the friend of God in Scripture twice that God Himself never said that he was His friend in the book of Genesis.

Moses also walked in fellowship with God and so closely to God in his relationship with God that God Himself said that they talked together as friends. Exodus 33:11 is God's word that says, **So the LORD spoke to Moses face to face, as a man speaks to his friend....** God elaborated on this friendship that He and Moses enjoyed in Numbers 12:6: **Then He said, "Hear now My words: If there is a prophet among you, I, the LORD, make Myself known to him in a vision; I speak to him in a dream. Not so with my servant Moses; He is faithful in all My house. I speak with him face to face."** This is an amazing friendship.

Moses' footsteps of friendship with God lead to something no-one else has ever experienced on this earth. Some have had visions of God but Moses saw God in person; true, he was not allowed to look at God's face because to do so would mean that he would then die but he did see God's glory manifested in God's backward parts as

He passed by. From John 4:24 we know that God is Spirit, not flesh, so we can only imagine what Moses saw. But, let's read the whole story from Genesis 33:12 to 23: **Then Moses said to the LORD, "See, You say to me, 'Bring up this people.' But You have not let me know whom You will send with me. Yet You have said, 'I know you by name, and you have also found grace in My sight. Now therefore, I pray, if I have found grace in Your sight, show me now Your way, that I may know You and that I may find grace in Your sight. And consider that this nation is Your people." And He said, "My Presence will go with you, and I will give you rest." Then he said to Him, "If Your Presence does not go with us, do not bring us up from here. For how then will it be known that Your people and I have found grace in Your sight, except You go with us? So we shall be separate, Your people and I, from all the people who are upon the face of the earth." So the LORD said to Moses, "I will also do this thing that you have spoken; for you have found grace in My sight, and I know you by name." And he** said, "Please, show me Your glory." Then He said, "I will make all My goodness pass before you, and I will proclaim the name of the LORD before you. I will be gracious to whom I will be gracious, and I will have compassion on whom I will have compassion." But He said, "You cannot see My face; for no man shall see Me, and live." And the LORD said, "Here is a place by Me, and you shall stand on the rock. So it shall be, while My glory passes by, that I will put you in the cleft of the rock, and will cover you with My hand while I pass by. Then I will take away My hand, and you shall see My back; but My face shall not be seen." This is an amazing example of God's footsteps of friendship as He walked past Moses so that Moses could see His glory.

Jesus' apostles had the tremendous experience of being called the friends of Jesus. Jesus said in John 15:14 & 15, **You are my friends, if ye do whatever I command you. No longer do I call you servants, for the servant does not know what his master is doing: but I have called you friends, for all things that I have heard from**

My Father I have made known to you. The footsteps of friendship with God means the revelation of truth from God. Jesus called them friends because servants only do as they are told without having to know the plans, purposes and directions of the master. However, the friends of the master are let in on the personal plans and purposes of the master. This is why Jesus called His disciples His friends. They walked together as friends, learning all that God wanted them to know so that years after Jesus' death and resurrection they could write these things down for us in what we now call the New Testament of the Bible.

Friendship with God is determined by trust that leads to our obedience to Him. If we are to walk in footsteps of friendship with God, we must trust Him and walk in implicit obedience to His will. The old hymn by Hahn H. Sammis, Trust and Obey, carries the keys to walking in footsteps of friendship with God. Verse 4 and the beginning of the chorus say, "*But we never can prove, The delights of His love, Until all on the altar we lay. For the favor He shows, And the joy He bestows, Are for them who will trust and obey. Trust and obey for there's no other way...".* Remember that God called Moses as a friend because he was faithful in all God's house.

Let us look at some of the characteristics of this walk of friendship. A friend is committed to the death. John 15:13 says, **Greater love has no one than this, than to lay down one's life for his friends**. Luke 12:4 also says, **And I say to you My friends, do not be afraid of those who kill the body, and after that have no more that they can do.** This is commitment to the death but as a friend, Jesus did that for us first of all. Romans 5:8 states, **But God demonstrates His own love toward us, in that while we were still sinners, Christ died for us.** The footsteps of friendship with God is a total commitment to Him above all else even as Jesus is totally committed to us.

We need to understand that correction by a friend is good. Proverbs 27:6 tell us, **Faithful are the wounds of a friend, But the kisses of an enemy are deceitful.** This is talking about rebukes and corrections made by a friend in order to cause us to walk uprightly. Taking correction or rebukes from anyone is difficult but the wise person will accept them and learn by them because the friend who does so is only trying to help us. Proverbs 27:17 says, **As iron sharpens iron, So a man sharpens the countenance of his friend.** Appreciate the correction of a friend, especially when that friend is the Lord God.

Proverbs 27:9 says, **Ointment and perfume delight the heart, And the sweetness of a man's friend gives delight by hearty counsel.** The generous loving counsel given by a friend is a delight to one's being. Good advice from a friend is a great blessing of friendship. Friendship with God means that His counsel will be sweet and delightful to us as His friends.

Friendship with the Lord means that your friendship with anything contrary to God and His will is cancelled in your life. James 4:4 warns us, **Adulterers and adulteresses! Do you not know that friendship with the world is enmity with God? Whoever therefore wants to be a friend of the world makes himself an enemy of God.** Anyone who is friend with the world system cannot be a friend of God. Remember that this world and all that is in it will soon be gone and only our relationship with Almighty God will really matter. Our friendship with God must be above all else. If we walk in footsteps of friendship with God we put nothing or no-one else ahead of Him

In conclusion, the walk of friendship footsteps with God are the footsteps that take the footsteps of fellowship to its highest level. God has done His part by reaching out through the death of Jesus, the Son of God, on a cross to be our Friend. We do our part by walking in obedience to God. This does not mean that we do not fail but it does mean that we take our failures immediately to God and we walk in restored fellowship with Him which was obtained and completed at the cross. God is reaching out to each one of us to deny ourselves and walk in His footsteps as His friend.

Chapter Four   Footsteps Of Faithfulness

God told the Israelites, after they had left Egypt, to walk after the Lord God. Deuteronomy 13:4 says, **You shall walk after the LORD your God and fear Him, and keep His commandments and obey His voice, and you shall serve Him and hold fast to Him.** God was requesting them, in fact requiring them, to walk in faithfulness with Him. Nothing else would satisfy His holy nature.

There are 5 aspects of these footsteps:

a.   **fear Him**

b.   **keep His commandments**

c.   **obey His voice**

d.   **serve Him**

e.   **hold fast to Him**

These are a description of the nature of faithfulness towards the Lord God. We are to have a healthy awesome respect and awe of the One who created us and holds our breath in His hands. In Job 12:10, of God Job said, **In whose hand *is* the life of every living thing, And the**

breath of all mankind? I have heard a mother upset with her child say, "I brought you into the world and I can take you out." While she does not actually plan on following through with that threat, God is indeed quite capable of doing so and if God is angry with someone His judgment is sure. God is a just judge. Psalm 7:11 says, **And God is angry *with the wicked* every day.** Therefore, obeying the commands of God becomes very easy and logical when you understand the greatness of God. This leads to the next step of obeying God's voice as He directs us. Therefore we will serve Him and hold fast to Him because we cannot do it on our own.

We are to walk in faithfulness to God because the Lord God is already walking in faithfulness towards us. Psalm 36:5 declares, **Your mercy, O LORD, is in the heavens; Your faithfulness reaches to the clouds.** In fact, 2 Timothy 2:13 assures us, **If we are faithless, He remains faithful; He cannot deny Himself.** We sing songs like "Great Is Thy Faithfulness" and "Faithful One, So Unchanging" because God always walks in faithfulness.

We need to define faithfulness. The dictionary has these definitions of "faithful":

1. True or trustworthy in the performance of duty, the fulfillment of promises or obligations, etc.: loyal

2. Worthy of belief or confidence; truthful

3. True in detail or accurate in description

Another dictionary says: Loyal, constant…, conscientious; trustworthy, true to fact…accurate.

The Hebrew word for faithfulness is "emunah", meaning "firmness, stability, faithfulness, fidelity, conscientiousness, steadiness and certainty". All of these are characteristics of God's footsteps of faithfulness. They are all also characteristics of the footsteps we are to take when we walk with God in footsteps of faithfulness. God is faithful to His covenants to those who are recipients of His promises. God wants us to walk in faithfulness to Him as well.

Let us look at God's footsteps of faithfulness. In Deuteronomy 7:9 we read, **Therefore know that the LORD your God, He is God, the faithful God who keeps**

covenant and mercy for thousand generations with those who love Him and keep His commandments; and He repays those who hate Him to their face, to destroy them. He will not be slack with him who hates Him; He will repay him to his face. Note that God's faithfulness is to thousands of generations, or in other words, forever. When God declares His faithfulness to a covenant He will not and cannot because of His faithful nature ever go back on that covenant no matter what anyone else does.

His word can be trusted for all time. That is why we find comfort and assurance in the words of 1 Corinthians 1:9: **God is faithful, by whom you were called into the fellowship of His Son, Jesus Christ our Lord.** Therefore, we can testify to all of God's faithfulness with total confidence. Hebrews 10:23 encourages us to maintain our trust in the faithfulness of God: **Let us hold fast the confession of our hope without wavering, for He who promised is faithful.** This means that God always keeps His end of the bargain: He cannot and will not fail. God's directions to us are faithful. Psalm 119:86a says, **All Your commandments are faithful...**

The servant of Abraham had this testimony in Genesis 24:48: **And I bowed my head and worshiped the LORD God of my master Abraham who had lead me in the way of truth to take the daughter of my master's brother for his son.** God had been faithful to walk with this servant of Abraham to find the bride for Isaac that God wanted for him. The servant responded with worship.

God's commandments are His directions to people for their good and the consequences of obeying or disobeying them will be fulfilled in faithfulness. God's leading may not always be fun and games but it is always a good and faithful way and will result in good for those who follow His leading. Romans 8:28 promises, **And we know that all things work together for good to those who love God, to those who are the called according to *His* purpose.**

God's discipline of His children is faithful and good. Psalm 119:75 may surprise many: **I know, O LORD, that**

Your judgments are right, And that in faithfulness You have afflicted me. This is talking about loving discipline from God to His children who have failed to obey Him. Hebrews 12:576 explains it this way: **And have you forgotten the exhortation which speaks to you as to sons: "My son, do not despise the chastening of the LORD, Nor be discouraged when you are rebuked by Him; For whom the LORD loves He chastens, And scourges every son whom He receives."** Godly discipline is loving faithful discipline and is for our good.

God's testimonies are faithful because He walks in faithfulness. Psalm 119:138 states, **Your testimonies, which You have commanded, Are righteous and very faithful.** The Hebrew word for "testimonies", eda, can mean assembly, company, multitude, people, swarm, testimonies or witness. The idea behind this word seems to be that a large group of people or things can be witness to something and testify of it. That God commanded testimonies is interesting in the light of Acts 1:8: **But you shall receive power when the Holy Spirit has come upon you; and**

you shall be witnesses to Me in Jerusalem, and in all Judea and Samaria and to the end of the earth. God has commanded that those who have witnessed the truth of God would spread it to the whole world. These testimonies are righteous and faithful because they are of God who is righteous and faithful.

God is faithful to forgive our wrongdoings if we put our trust in the Lord Jesus Christ and confess our sins to Him. 1 John 1:9 assures us, **If we confess our sins, He is faithful and just to forgive us our sins and to cleanse us from all unrighteousness**. This is the first step we take in walking with God in the footsteps of faithfulness.

God is faithful to keep His faithful followers on into eternity. 1 Corinthians 1:4-9 are the words of the apostle Paul: **I thank my God always concerning you for the grace of God which was given to you by Christ Jesus, that you were enriched in every thing by Him in all utterance and all knowledge, even as the testimony of Christ was confirmed in you, so that you come short in no gift, who you may be blameless in the day of our**

Lord Jesus Christ. God is faithful, by whom you were called into the fellowship of His Son, Jesus Christ our Lord. In other words, God is faithful to save you and to keep you until the end by His love and power through His great grace. 1 Thessalonians 5:23 & 24 follow on with this prayer of Paul: **Now may the God of peace Himself sanctify you completely; and may your whole spirit, soul, and body be preserved blameless at the coming of our Lord Jesus Christ. He who calls you is faithful, who also will do it.**

Paul's testimony to Timothy in 2 Timothy 1:12 is, **For this reason I also suffer these things; nevertheless I am not ashamed, for I know whom I have believed and am persuaded that He is able to keep what I have committed to Him until that Day.** The question is not if God is faithful to keep us but, rather, are we willing to stay faithful to Him and trust Him in all things.

You can be confident that God's faithfulness will not let you go through more than you can handle. 1 Corinthians 10:13 assures us, **No temptation has overtaken you**

except such as is common to man; but God is faithful, who will not allow you to be tempted beyond what you are able, but with the temptation will also make the way of escape, that you may be able to bear it. In ancient thought, "temptation" and "trial" were the same; you can substitute the word "trial" in this verse everywhere "temptation" is written and it would be accurate. God will not allow you to go through any temptation or trial that He will not give you the ability to go through in victory.

God is faithful to protect us from Satan and his forces. 2 Thessalonians 3:3 bring us this confidence: **But the Lord is faithful, who will establish you and guard you from the evil one.** As we walk with God in the pathway of faithfulness God establishes us and protects us from the enemy.

The Lord God, then, is faithful in all His ways and walks the path of faithfulness continually . Psalm 36:5 boldly states, **Your mercy, O LORD, is in the heavens; Your faithfulness reaches to the clouds.** There is no limit to the faithfulness of God.

The challenge is for us to walk in paths of faithfulness with our faithful God. David' request in 1 Samuel 26:23 was, **May the LORD repay every man for his righteousness and his faithfulness...** Some people want people repaid for the wrong they have done but in this case David wanted those who were righteousness to be repaid by God for their faithfulness.

David, as king, looked for righteous and faithful people to serve under him. Psalm 101:6 are the words of king David: **My eyes shall be on the faithful of the land, that they may dwell with me; he who walks in a perfect way, he shall serve me.** Sometimes it is hard to find faithful people. Proverbs 20:6 addresses this problem. **Most men will proclaim each his own goodness, but who can find a faithful man?**

God is looking for faithfulness in us, as His children. 1 Corinthians 4:2 puts it clearly: **Moreover it is required in stewards that one be found faithful.** Peter, in 1 Peter 4:10 says, **As each one has received a gift, minister it to one another, as good stewards of the manifold grace of**

God. All believers have received at least one gift from God and is required to be a good faithful steward of what God has invested in them

Faithfulness is mandatory in church leaders. In 1 Timothy 3:1-12 we are given the requirements of bishops or elders and deacons (church leaders) which are aspects of faithfulness to God and the church. In verse 11, even the deacons' wives are required to be faithful if their husbands are to serve as deacons – **Likewise, their wives must be reverent, not slanderers, temperate, faithful in all things.**

Footsteps of faithfulness are progressive. Luke 16:10 & 11 explains, **He who is faithful in what is least is faithful also in much; and he who is unjust in what is least is unjust also in much. Therefore if you have not been faithful in the unrighteous mammon, who will commit to your trust the true riches?** God always starts testing us with small things and if we can be faithful in small things He will give us greater and greater things for which we are to be responsible. The least responsibility seems to be money. Scripture is very clear as to how we are to handle the money God has entrusted to us. If we cannot be faithful in handling our money the way God has directed, He may not entrust you with much else for His cause.

Paul was grateful for the honour of being considered faithful enough to entrust him with ministering the gospel to the Gentiles. 1 Timothy 1:12 is Paul's testimony of gratitude: **And I thank Christ Jesus our Lord who has enabled me, because He counted me faithful, putting me into the ministry.** Note that the enabling to minister effectively came from God because of the faithfulness of His servant.

Faithfulness to God means commitment to God, His Word, His directions in our lives, His holiness and His glory. Proverbs 16:17 says, **The highway** (or path) **of the upright is to depart from evil; He who keeps his way preserves his soul.** Footsteps of faithfulness means total commitment to the Lord.

Faithfulness in us is developed as we yield to the Holy Spirit within us, letting His fruit grow to maturity in us. Galatians 5:22 & 23 reveal that one of the fruits of the Spirit is faithfulness: **But the fruit of the Spirit is love, joy, peace, longsuffering, kindness, goodness, <u>faithfulness</u>** (the emphasis is mine)**, gentleness, self-control. Against such there is no law.** Along with all the other fruit that we consider to be spiritual is faithfulness. It is only by God's grace and power that we can be faithful to God as He is to us.

Always remember that God walks in faithfulness and God wants us to walk in faithfulness with Him. God will reward those who walk in faithfulness: Psalm 31:23: **Oh, love the LORD, all you His saints! For the LORD preserves the faithful, and fully repays the proud person.** We have this assurance from God's Word in Proverbs 28:20: **A faithful man will abound with blessings...**

Chapter Five   Footsteps of Fortification

When considering these footsteps we need to be clear that God does not need to be fortified or protected. The question is, "How big is God?" or "How big is your God?" Deuteronomy 10:17 says, **For the LORD your God *is* God of gods and Lord of lords, the great God, mighty and awesome, who shows no partiality nor takes a bribe.** The Lord God is God over all so-called gods and Lord over all lords. He is mighty and awesome.

This is the One who created both heavens and earth. He is the creator of our universe and all the universes beyond our universe. Psalm 148:1-13 portray this: **Praise the LORD! Praise the LORD from the heavens; praise Him in the heights! Praise Him, all His angels; praise Him, all His hosts! Praise Him, sun and moon; praise Him, all you stars of light! Praise Him, you heavens of heavens, and you waters above the heavens! Let them praise the name of the LORD, for He commanded and they were created. He also established them forever** and ever; he made a decree which shall not pass away. Praise the LORD from the earth, you great sea creatures and all the depths; Fire and hail, snow and clouds; Stormy wind, fulfilling His word; Mountains and all hills; fruitful trees and all cedars; Beasts and all cattle; creeping things and flying fowl; Kings of the earth and all peoples; princes and all judges of the earth; Both young men and maidens; old men and children. Let them praise the name of the LORD, for His name alone is exalted; his glory is above the earth and heaven.

The greatness of God is found in Deuteronomy 4:39: **Therefore know this day, and consider it in your heart, that the LORD Himself is God in heaven above and on the earth beneath; there is no other.** Jeremiah 10:6 adds, **Inasmuch as there is none like You, O LORD (You are great, and Your name is great in might).** The words of Jehoshaphat in 2 Chronicles 20:6 say, ..."**O LORD God of our fathers, *are* You not God in heaven, and do You *not* rule over all the kingdoms of the nations, and in Your** hand is there not power and might, so that no one is able to withstand You?"

When God walks in the footsteps of fortification, He is being the fortress and protection for others, not Himself. Deuteronomy 23:14 says, **For the LORD your God walks in the midst of your camp, to deliver you and give your enemies over to you; therefore your camp shall be holy, that He may see no unclean thing among you, and turn away from you**. God walks unseen in the midst of His people. God does so in order to deliver His people and overcome the enemies of God's people.

We need to define fortification if we are to understand these footsteps. The dictionary definition is "defensive work". Note that this is not an offensive work as with a weapon but, rather, a defensive work, such as a protective wall that keeps out the enemy.

Let's look at the footsteps of fortification in more detail. When we walk with God in footsteps of fortification, we are walking in His protection and fortification. Psalm 18:2 puts it clearly: **The LORD is my rock and my fortress and** my deliverer; my God, my strength, in whom I will trust; my shield and the horn of my salvation, my stronghold.

He is our solid Rock on whom we stand. He is our deliverer when we get into trouble. He is our strength. He is our shield that shelters us from attack. He is our horn of salvation - the horn spoke of power and authority, kind of like facing a charging bull with his head down and horns aimed at you.

He is our fortress in whom we can find protection - Proverbs 18:10 says, **The name of the LORD *is* a strong tower; The righteous run to it and are safe.** He is our stronghold that can withstand any onslaught. Romans 8:31 declares, **What then shall we say to these things? If God *is* for us, who *can be* against us?**

Of Biblical examples of God's footsteps of fortification, the story of three Hebrew teenagers is one of my favourites. Daniel 3:23-25 tells part of the story. **And these three men, Shadrach, Meshach, and Abed-Nego, fell down bound into the midst of the burning fiery furnace. Then King Nebuchadnezzar was astonished;**

and he rose in haste and spoke, saying to his counselors, "Did we not cast three men bound into the midst of the fire?" They answered and said to the king, "True, O king." "Look!" he answered, "I see four men loose, walking in the midst of the fire; and they are not hurt, and the form of the fourth is like the Son of God."

This is one of the most well-known stories in the Bible. These three young teenagers named Hananiah, Mishael, and Azariah were taken captive from Judah to Babylon in the Babylonian captivity. They were renamed Shadrach, Meshach and Abed-Nego by King Nebuchadnezzar. They would not bow down and worship the idol that the king had set up for all to worship because they were true to God. The king was angry and had the smelting furnace heated seven times hotter than usual, probably over 1,000 degrees F. When the king looked in he saw three people walking around in the furnace in footsteps of fortification and the fourth one was "like the Son of God." When the three young men came out they were not singed and did not even smell of smoke. The Lord had been walking in the midst of the fiery furnace with them with footsteps of fortification protecting them.

In Judges 2:1-6 we read something unusual: **Then the Angel of the LORD came up from Gilgal to Bochim, and said: "I led you up from Egypt and brought you to the land of which I swore to your fathers; and I said, 'I will never break My covenant with you. And you shall make no covenant with the inhabitants of this land; you shall tear down their altars.' But you have not obeyed My voice. Why have you done this? Therefore I also said, 'I will not drive them out before you; but they shall be *thorns* in your side, and their gods shall be a snare to you.' " So it was, when the Angel of the LORD spoke these words to all the children of Israel, that the people lifted up their voices and wept. Then they called the name of that place Bochim** (Tears, because they had wept tears of repentance); **and they sacrificed there to the LORD. And when Joshua had dismissed the people, the children of Israel went each to his own inheritance to possess the land.** The Angel of the LORD identifies

Himself here as the Lord God of Israel. Many believe that this Angel of the LORD was a pre-incarnate appearance of the Son of God who was named Jesus when He was born to Mary in Bethlehem. God said that it was He who led them out of Egypt and brought them to the promised land. It was He who made a covenant with them and would never break it. He told them that they had not obeyed Him and would face their enemies because they had not obeyed Him. God had walked with them in footsteps of fortification but they had not acknowledged Him and now would have to face the enemy alone. What a shock and disappointment to them, but it did not seem to matter too much to them later on because they did not continue in faithfulness to God after this pronouncement to them.

There are, therefore, requirements in order to walk in footsteps of fortification. Isaiah 54:17 tells us, **No weapon formed against you shall prosper, And every tongue which rises against you in judgment You shall condemn. This is the heritage of the servants of the LORD, And their righteousness is from Me," Says the**

LORD. The protection of the Lord is for those who are servants of the Lord. This means you must be serving the Lord. Serving means following the Lord as faithfully as possible.

The other requirement here is to be a child of God whose righteousness is from God. Romans 3:10 says, **As it is written: " There is none righteous, no, not one;** so that means that all of our own self-righteousness is to no avail. However if you have accepted Jesus Christ as your Saviour and have committed your life to Him, you are set free from sin. Romans 6:18 goes on to say, **And having been set free from sin, you became slaves of righteousness.** You cannot earn the right to walk in the footsteps of fortification; you have to obtain it by putting your faith in the Lord Jesus Christ.

Trusting in the Lord is paramount to walking in the footsteps of fortification. David said in Psalm 56:3, **Whenever I am afraid, I will trust in You.** David had reason to be fearful. For several years king Saul was out to kill him with his armies and friends. David did not feel safe anywhere in the land of Israel. David found his protection by trusting in the Lord.

Years before when David was much younger we find in 1 Samuel 16:12 & 13 that the prophet Samuel had heard that Jesse had a son named David, **So he sent and brought him in. Now he was ruddy, with bright eyes, and good-looking. And the LORD said, "Arise, anoint him; for this is the one!" Then Samuel took the horn of oil and anointed him in the midst of his brothers; and the Spirit of the LORD came upon David from that day forward. So Samuel arose and went to Ramah.** David must have held this promise of God in his heart all those years in spite of natural fear.

Isaiah lived in troublesome times and could have feared for his life. However Isaiah said in Isaiah 12:2, **Behold, God *is* my salvation, I will trust and not be afraid; ' For YAH, the LORD, *is* my strength and song; He also has become my salvation.'** Isaiah chose to trust God and not be afraid. In fact he trusted God as his strength and even chose to sing the Lord's praises. Not being afraid was a choice that he made as he trusted in the Lord. Now, that's walking in the footsteps of fortification with God.

God has an end-time promise of fortification for His people. Zechariah 9:9-17 states, **"Rejoice greatly, O daughter of Zion! Shout, O daughter of Jerusalem! Behold, your King is coming to you; He *is* just and having salvation, Lowly and riding on a donkey, A colt, the foal of a donkey. I will cut off the chariot from Ephraim And the horse from Jerusalem; The battle bow shall be cut off. He shall speak peace to the nations; His dominion shall be 'from sea to sea, And from the River to the ends of the earth.' "As for you also, Because of the blood of your covenant, I will set your prisoners free from the waterless pit. Return to the stronghold, You prisoners of hope. Even today I declare That I will restore double to you. For I have bent Judah, My *bow,* Fitted the bow with Ephraim, And raised up your sons, O Zion, Against your sons, O Greece, And made you like the sword of a mighty man." Then the LORD will be seen over them, And His arrow will go forth like** lightning. The Lord GOD will blow the trumpet, And go with whirlwinds from the south. The LORD of hosts will defend them; They shall devour and subdue with slingstones. They shall drink and roar as if with wine; They shall be filled with blood like basins, Like the corners of the altar. The LORD their God will save them in that day, As the flock of His people. For they shall be like the jewels of a crown, Lifted like a banner over His land --- For how great is its goodness And how great its beauty! Grain shall make the young men thrive, And new wine the young women.**

Zechariah, in this portion of Scripture, prophesies first of all of the triumphant entry of Jesus into Jerusalem as John described in John 12:12 & 13: **The next day a great multitude that had come to the feast, when they heard that Jesus was coming to Jerusalem, took branches of palm trees and went out to meet Him, and cried out: " Hosanna! ' Blessed is He who comes in the name of the LORD!' The King of Israel!"** Then Zechariah jumps forward at least 2,000 years or more and portrays the coming of Messiah Yeshua, Jesus Christ, to overthrow the wicked and set up His kingdom. The next part is a promise to set the prisoners free from the waterless pit. This is a spiritual pit that the people had gotten into because of their disobedience to God. Their rescue is stated, **Because of the blood of your covenant**, a look at the importance of the death of Jesus on the cross.

The blood of Jesus removed the penalty of sin. Romans 3:24-26 says, **being justified freely by His grace through the redemption that is in Christ Jesus, whom God set forth *as* a propitiation by His blood, through faith, to demonstrate His righteousness, because in His forbearance God had passed over the sins that were previously committed, to demonstrate at the present time His righteousness, that He might be just and the justifier of the one who has faith in Jesus.**

Hebrews 13:20 & 21 go on to say, **Now may the God of peace who brought up our Lord Jesus from the dead, that great Shepherd of the sheep, through the blood of the everlasting covenant, make you complete** in every good work to do His will, working in you what is well pleasing in His sight, through Jesus Christ, to whom *be* glory forever and ever. Amen.

The call after this is to "**Return to the stronghold.**" This is not a physical stronghold. This is referring to the stronghold that is in Christ Jesus through the blood of His covenant. The rest that follows is God's promise of great blessing to those who take up His call to return to Him and walk in the footsteps of fortification with Him.

Zechariah 10:12 is a prophetic word for those who trust in the Lord and walk in the footsteps of fortification with God. He promises us, **"So I will strengthen them in the LORD, And they shall walk up and down in His name,"** **Says the LORD.** God will strengthen those who walk up and down in His name in footsteps of faithfulness.

God provides comfort with His protecting presence as He walks with us. Deuteronomy 31:8 is the promise of God's presence to guide and protect Israel - **And the LORD, He *is* the One who goes before you. He will be with you, He will not leave you nor forsake you; do not**

fear nor be dismayed." This promise was given to Joshua by Moses. This same promise is ours today.

Psalm 23:3 can be our testimony: **Yea, though I walk through the valley of the shadow of death, I will fear no evil; For You *are* with me; Your rod and Your staff, they comfort me.** This well known psalm shows that God walks with us to comfort us in the hard times. We need not fear because our fortification is with us as we walk with Him.

Our assurance is found in the words of Jesus in Matthew 28:18-20: **And Jesus came and spoke to them, saying, "All authority has been given to Me in heaven and on earth. Go therefore and make disciples of all the nations, baptizing them in the name of the Father and of the Son and of the Holy Spirit, teaching them to observe all things that I have commanded you; <u>and lo, I am with you always, *even* to the end of the age." Amen.</u>**

Psalm 7:10 puts it this way: **My defense *is* of God, Who saves the upright in heart.** Also, let us remember the promise of God in Psalm 37:39 & 40: **But the salvation of the righteous is from the LORD; he is their strength in** the time of trouble. And the LORD shall help them and deliver them; he shall deliver them from the wicked, and save them, because they trust in Him.

We have God's promise in 2 Thessalonians 3:3: **But the Lord is faithful, who will establish you and guard *you* from the evil one,** so we can walk confidently with Almighty God in footsteps of fortification.

Chapter Five   Footsteps of Following To Fruitfulness

David said in Psalm 63:8, **"My soul follows close behind You; Your right hand upholds me."** David's strong desire was to follow closely behind the steps of the Lord. David knew that when He followed close to the Lord, the Lord's right hand would uphold him. The right hand always signified power and authority. When we walk close to God His power and authority are with us.

Matthew 7:13 & 14 say, **Enter by the narrow gate; for wide is the gate and broad is the way that leads to destruction, and there are many who go in by it. Because narrow is the gate and difficult is the way which leads to life, and there are few who find it.** The footsteps of God lead through a narrow gate and difficult path. This pathway that God leads in, though it may be narrow and difficult, leads to real life. In fact, Jesus said in John 14:6, **"I am the way, the truth, and the life. No one comes to the Father except through Me."** Jesus is both the pathway and the life as well as the truth. God's footsteps always lead us to Jesus Christ.

Fruitfulness is in the heart of God. God's goal for the physical world that He created was fruitfulness. Vegetation was to be fruitful and multiply. We read in Genesis 1:11 &12, **Then God said, "Let the earth bring forth grass, the herb that yields seed, and the fruit tree that yields fruit according to its kind, whose seed is in itself, on the earth"; and it was so. And the earth brought forth grass, the herb that yields seed according to its kind, and the tree that yields fruit, whose seed is itself according to its kind. And God saw that it was good.**

The sea life and fowl of the air God created to be fruitful. Genesis 1:20 & 21 tell us, **Then God said, "Let the waters abound with an abundance of living creatures, and let birds fly above the earth across the face of the firmament of the heavens." So God created great sea creatures and every living thing that moves, with which the waters abounded, according to their** kind, and every winged bird according to its kind. And God saw that it was good.

God created animals on the earth to be fruitful as well. Genesis 1:24 & 25 says, **Then God said, "Let the earth bring forth the living creature according to its kind: cattle and creeping thing and beast of the earth, each according to its kind"; and it was so. And God made the beast of the earth according to its kind, cattle according to its kind, and everything that creeps on the earth according to its kind. And God saw that it was good.**

Finally, we read in Genesis 1:27 & 28, **So God created man in His own image; in the image of God He created him; male and female He created them. Then God blessed them, and God said to them, "Be fruitful and multiply; fill the earth and subdue it; have dominion over the fish of the sea, over the birds of the air, and over every living thing that moves on the earth.**

It is very evident that God created all living things to be fruitful and produce after its own kind. This is called THE

LAW OF THE HARVEST or the law of sowing and reaping. It is true in botany and in biology as everyone knows.

God's goal in the moral and spiritual realm is fruitfulness as well. The law of the harvest in Galatians 6:7 states, **"Do not be deceived, God is not mocked; for whatever a man sows, that he will also reap."** Galatians 6:8 explains in greater depth. **For he who sows to the flesh will of the flesh reap corruption, but he who sows to the Spirit will of the Spirit reap everlasting life.**

Psalm 126:5 & 6 shares encouragement to those who struggle in their effort to be fruitful. **Those who sow in tears Shall reap in joy. He who continually goes forth weeping, Bearing seed for sowing, Shall doubtless come again with rejoicing, Bringing His sheaves with him.**

The degree to which we reap in fruitfulness is determined by the degree to which we sow. 2 Corinthians 9:6 puts it this way: **But this I say: He who sows sparingly will also reap sparingly, and he who sows bountifully will also reap bountifully.** I know of a farmer who complained to his neighbour that his corn field was not producing a good crop of corn. The stalks of corn grew in little patches and although the corn was doing well, there were few plants. The neighbour had a field of corn beside this farmer's field and it was a bountiful harvest. The neighbour asked the farmer how he planted the corn. The farmer replied that as he started to go around the field with the seed drill he was shocked to see how much seed was disappearing into the ground and so he set the seed drill down to only let much less corn seed fall through the tubes to the ground below. The neighbour laughed, "You did not plant enough seed. You only harvest what you plant".

This law of the harvest is a principle. A law becomes a principle if it is found all through the Scripture and is not unique to one time period. An example is the law of tithing which began with Abraham and Melchizedek, priest of the Most High God long before it was incorporated into the law given to Moses and then is again mentioned in the church period in Hebrews 7:8. Therefore it is a principle covering all time. So it is with the law of the harvest.

God's footsteps that lead to fruitfulness are steps that follow from His nature. He walks in love because He is love. 1 John 4:7 states, **Beloved, let us love one another, for love is of God; and everyone who loves is born of God and knows God.**

He walks in holiness because He is holy. Psalm 99:9 exhorts us, **Exalt the Lord our God, And worship at His holy hill; For the LORD our God is holy.**

He walks in mercy because He is merciful. God says in Hebrews 8:12, **For I will be merciful to their unrighteousness, and their sins and lawless deeds I will remember no more.**

He walks in grace because He is gracious. Psalm 103:8 tells us, **The LORD is merciful and gracious, Slow to anger, and abounding in mercy.**

He walks in goodness because He is always good. Romans 2:4 declares, **Or do you despise the riches of His goodness, forbearance, and longsuffering, not knowing that the goodness of God leads you to repentance?**

He is compassionate, longsuffering and truthful. We read in Psalm 86:15, **But You, O Lord, are a God full of compassion, and gracious, Longsuffering and abundant in mercy and truth.**

All of God's footsteps follow the characteristics of His nature and they lead to fruitfulness in those characteristics for our good and His glory. Our amazing God leads according to His amazing characteristics in amazing ways and places.

Mankind is called to walk in fruitfulness. Specifically God calls us to walk in His footsteps that lead to fruitfulness in Psalm 23:3. **He restores my soul; He leads me in the paths of righteousness For His name's sake.** Note that His footsteps lead us in paths for His name's sake, not our name's sake. Sometimes we want to follow God so that we will be exalted. This will not work for God must be exalted in all things. If we are exalted at all it is because of God's great mercy and not because we deserve anything special.

God leads us in the path that is right for each one of us. Isaiah 48:17 says, **Thus says the LORD, your**

Redeemer, The Holy One of Israel: **"I am the LORD your God, Who teaches you to profit, Who leads you by the way you should go."** The Lord God wants His people to profit or prosper so as we follow His footsteps He teaches us how to be successful. Understand that success is measured by God's definition, not by what the world considers success. His footsteps lead us in the way that is good for us to go.

Jesus often called to people, **"Follow Me."** as in Matthew 4:19; 8:22; 9:9; 16:24; 19:21, etc. so we can also call these footsteps our "Follow Me Footsteps".

It is dangerous not to follow the footsteps of the Lord that He has given for you to follow. Ezekiel 13:3 warned the false prophets, **Thus says the Lord God: "Woe to the foolish prophets, who follow their own spirit and have seen nothing!"** Woe means sadness and terrible circumstances as a result of following their own footsteps instead of God's.

Proverbs 20:24 are very interesting: **A man's steps are of the LORD; How then can a man understand his**

own way? If the Lord is showing us the footsteps we are to take, we cannot rationalize the way that we should go. We need to hear the heartbeat of the Master and follow His footsteps that will lead to fruitfulness in our lives.

Following the Lord's footsteps is a decision and a deliberate choice. Luke 9:22:3 tells us, **Then He** (Jesus) **said to them all, "If anyone desires to come after Me, let him deny himself, and take up his cross daily and follow Me.** We choose to follow by putting aside our own plans and paths that we would like to follow. Then we take up our own cross (that which leads to our own crucified life, dying to self so we can be alive to God) and follow the Lord.

Of the good king Josiah, in the days of the kings of Judah, 2 Kings 23:3 says, **Then the king stood by a pillar and made a covenant before the LORD, to follow the LORD and keep His commandments and His testimonies and His statutes, with all his heart and all his soul, to perform the words of this covenant that were written in this book. And all the people took a stand for the covenant.**

Following the footsteps of God means that you not follow anyone else's footstep. In Matthew 10:37-39, Jesus said, **He who loves father or mother more than Me is not worthy of Me. And he who loves son or daughter more than Me is not worthy of Me. And he who does not take up his cross and follow after Me is not worthy of Me. He who finds his life will lose it, and he who loses his life for My sake will find it**. It is dangerous to follow anyone's directions, even if they tell you that God told them that something specific is what you are to do, unless God confirms it in your own heart first. Many stories of sorrow and disaster have resulted from such errors in judgment.

Following God's footsteps means that you will be where God is. In John 12:26 Jesus said, **If anyone serves Me, let him follow Me; and where I am, there My servant will be also. If anyone serves Me, him My Father will honour.** You cannot follow Someone if you are not there with Him. People who are truly following the Lord will be where He is. If the Lord's presence is not in a place, they will not be there either. Some people stay in church where

:e of God has not been manifested for years.

o start earnestly seeking God for Him to show

. ...dst or get out and go to a fellowship where the presence of God is sensed. Sometimes God will direct people to intercede in prayer until revival comes but sometimes God will tell them that the glory has departed and it is time for them to depart too. Once in a while God will direct to go and start an new ministry for His glory. It is far easier to give birth than to raise the dead. However, at no time should people become arrogant and prideful but should have open hearts and arms to all other believers. God loves them too.

Following God's footsteps to fruitfulness is an individual path that is personal to each one. John 21:20-22 gives the instruction to Peter at the Last Supper that Jesus had with His disciples. **Then Peter, turning around, saw the disciple whom Jesus loved following, who also had leaned on His breast at the supper, and said, "Lord, who is the one who betrays You?" Peter, seeing him, said to Jesus, but Lord, what about this man?" Jesus** said to him, **"If I will that he remain till I come, what is that to you? You follow Me."** Each one has his own path.

Following in footsteps to fruitfulness means to follow the Lord eagerly, in service to Him wholeheartedly. In Joshua 22:4 **Joshua commanded the people, But take careful heed to do the commandment and the law which Moses the servant of the LORD commanded you, to love the LORD your God, to walk in all His ways, to keep His commandments, to hold fast to Him, and to serve Him with all your heart and with all your soul.**

Following in footsteps to fruitfulness means obedience to the Lord in every way possible. 2 Kings 18:5 & 6 describe King Hezekiah: **He trusted in the LORD God of Israel, so that after him was none like him among all the kings of Judah, nor who were before him. For he held fast to the LORD; he did not depart from following Him, but kept His commandments, which the LORD had commanded Moses**.

Following the footsteps to fruitfulness means focusing on the path ahead and the One who is leading, not looking around or back. In Luke 9:62 Jesus addressed a man wanting to follow Him: **But Jesus said to him, "No one, having put his hand to the plough, and looking back, is fit for the kingdom of God."**

There are several aspects of footsteps to fruitfulness that we need to look at. These footsteps encourage the building up of others. Romans 14:19 commands us, **Therefore let us pursue the things which make for peace and the things by which one may edify another.** (also see 1 Peter 2:21-24). These footsteps are footsteps of selflessness. Our spiritual lives are not about us as much as about the Lord and others. The old Sunday School chorus was right when it rang out, "Jesus and Others and You. What a wonderful way to spell JOY. Jesus and Others and You in the life of each girl and each boy. J is for Jesus who must take first place. O is for others you meet face to face. Y is for you and whatever you do, just put yourself last and spell JOY."

Love and spiritual gifts are to be sought on these footsteps of following to fruitfulness. 1 Corinthians 14:1 tells us, **Pursue love, and desire spiritual gifts, but especially that you may prophesy.** Some people are afraid of the spiritual gifts and do the opposite. Jesus promised us in Luke 11:13, **"If you then, being evil, know how to give good gifts to your children, how much more will your heavenly Father give the Holy Spirit to those who ask Him!"** There is no need to fear. God will not allow you to get something false if you ask Him for what He desires you to have and tells you to ask for it.

The footsteps of following to fruitfulness is good for all. 1 Thessalonians 5:15 says, **See that no one renders evil for evil to anyone, but always pursue what is good both for yourselves and for all.** God is good and goodness flows from Him and all His footsteps. When we walk in God's footsteps we walk in goodness to all.

Righteousness, godliness, faith, love, patience and gentleness line the pathway of these footsteps. 1 Timothy 6:11 encourages us with, **But you, O man of God, flee these things and pursue righteousness, godliness, faith, love, patience, gentleness.** We should not be surprised because these are the attributes or characteristics of God. They are to be ours as well.

Peace with all holiness comes with these footsteps. Hebrews 12:14 explains, **Pursue peace with all people, and holiness, without which no one will see the Lord.** Peace is the plan and purpose of God for all mankind. Jesus said in John 16:33, **"These things I have spoken to you, that in Me you may have peace. In the world you will have tribulation; but be of good cheer, I have overcome the world."**

Holiness is essential in us. 1 Peter 1:5 & 6 say, **but as He who called you is holy, you also be holy in all your conduct, because it is written, "Be holy, for I am holy."** When we look at God and His holiness this statement is scary. It seems impossible.

How can we be holy as God is holy? It looks hopeless. Ephesians 4:24 helps to encourage us in this regard: **and that you put on the new man which was created according to God, in true righteousness and holiness.** God made us new people when we accepted

Christ as our Saviour and the new nature is a nature of righteousness and holiness.

The apostle Paul wrote in 2 Corinthians 7:1, **Therefore, having these promises, beloved, let us cleanse ourselves from all filthiness of the flesh and spirit, perfecting holiness in the fear of God.** We cleanse ourselves by confession of sin as is said in 1 John 1:9: **If we confess our sins, He is faithful and just to forgive us *our* sins and to cleanse us from all unrighteousness.** The next step is to claim and walk toward purity in our lives, rather than focusing on the impurity of the flesh and trying to beat it. Focus on the good and not on the bad.

Romans 6:22 goes on to show that our holiness is God's production in us. **But now having been set free from sin, and having become slaves of God, you have your fruit to holiness, and the end, everlasting life.** Our responsibility is to run away from the unholy things to remain in the purity that God has for us. When we focus on the holiness of God as we walk in the following to fruitfulness footsteps of God and we will see that holiness is a fruit that is developed in our lives.

This is the pathway of the high calling of God in Jesus Christ as Philippians 3:14 says: **I press toward the goal for the prize of the upward call of God in Christ Jesus.** The high calling of God is what is referred to as the upward call of God. We are headed to a glorious eternity with our wonderful God and Saviour. We need to get that into our hearts and souls and rejoice in that fact. The life that we live on this earth is but a dim shadow of what is to come. The real living is what we experience with the Lord for that will take us into eternity to more than we could ever dream about.

These footsteps are only followed as you abide in Christ (keep connected to Him daily). Jesus said in John 15:4, **Abide in Me, and I in you. As the branch cannot bear fruit of itself, unless it abides in the vine, neither can you, unless you abide in Me.** Fruitfulness comes by keeping linked to the vine and Jesus said in John 14:1 that He is the vine.

The fruit of this walk is of the Holy Spirit in us. Galatians 5:22 & 23 explains, **But the fruit of the Spirit is love, joy, peace, longsuffering, kindness, goodness, faithfulness, gentleness, self-control. Against such there is no law.** These fruit are self-explanatory except for "longsuffering" which is better translated as "patience or endurance". We cannot walk this walk alone. God, the Holy Spirit in us, will lead us if we let Him work in us. We will have certain results if we walk in footsteps of following to fruitfulness letting God the Holy Spirit lead and direct.

These footsteps provide sufficiency in all things and peacefulness. Psalm 23:1-23 declares, **The Lord is my shepherd; I shall not want. He makes me to lie down in green pastures; He leads me beside the still waters. He restores my soul...** "I shall not want" can be paraphrased as "I shall have all I need." God may not give us all we want but will give us all that we need. 2 Corinthians 3:5 puts it this way: **Not that we are sufficient of ourselves to think of anything as being from ourselves, but our sufficiency is from God.**

Another result is that all condemnation is removed. Romans 8:1 says, **There is therefore now no condemnation to those who are in Christ Jesus, who do not walk according to the flesh, but according to the Spirit.** The Aramaic Translation of Romans 8:1 by George Lamsa, puts it this way: **There is therefore no condemnation to them who walk in the flesh after the Spirit of Jesus Christ.** I think this may be the most accurate translation. I am not sure, but I do like it. Guilt is gone. God holds nothing against us because Jesus took the sin and its consequences away by taking them on Himself. We walk in the unredeemed flesh but follow after the Spirit of Christ, the Holy Spirit.

We also find that good works are remembered and rewarded after our death. In Revelation 14:13 we read, **Then I heard a voice from heaven saying to me, "Write: Blessed are the dead who die in the Lord from now on." "Yes," says the Spirit, "that they may rest from their labours and their works follow them."** Jesus said in Matthew 16:27, **For the Son of Man will come in the glory**

of His Father with His angels, and then He will reward each according to his works. Although we are not saved by any works we do, we are rewarded for the works that we have done for God. We must be cautious that we do not try to receive glory in this life for our good works because if they are truly done for the Lord, they are only for His glory alone.

One amazing result is that God's righteousness will become ours through Jesus Christ. Psalm 85:13, speaking of the Lord, says, **Righteousness will go before Him, And shall make His footsteps our pathway.** The New Testament declaration is found in 2 Corinthians 5:21: **For He made Him who knew no sin to be sin for us, that we might become the righteousness of God in Him.** Not only has the righteousness of Christ been put to our account before God but we are declared to be His righteousness in Christ Jesus. God declares to the spiritual world that we are His righteousness. It is more than I can comprehend that we created beings, subject to imperfection and failure, can be the righteousness of God, all because we are in Christ Jesus!

Another result is that Jesus said He would go with us. Matthew 28:18-20 tell us, **And Jesus came and spoke to them, saying, "All authority has been given to Me in heaven and on earth. Go therefore and make disciples of all the nations, baptizing them in the name of the Father and of the Son and of the Holy Spirit, teaching them to observe all things that I have commanded you; and lo, I am with you always, *even* to the end of the age." Amen.** We can depend on Him to be there for us as we walk in His footsteps.

When things are going well, God is with you. When life is hard and things seem to be going downhill fast, God is with you. He will never leave you alone. He is right there loving you and reaching out to and for you.

If we walk in the footsteps of God that follow after His character and desires, we will definitely produce fruitfulness. One young man, many years ago, had turned his life over to Christ and after a few months was concerned that he did not seem to have any fruitfulness in His life for God. When he told me that he was doing his best to follow after God, I told him to ask those who knew him best to tell him if they saw any fruitfulness in his life. He did so and just as I suspected, they told him that there had been major changes in his life and in his attitude towards others. They saw fruitfulness coming out of his life of which he was not even aware. The fruit of walking this walk of following footsteps takes time to grow. Our fruit may appear to be unripe to us but it is the fruit of the Spirit developing in us and others will soon taste and see that God is good because of that fruit in our lives.

Walking in God's steps that follow to fruitfulness may seem unproductive to you. Others, however, see the glory of God in your life if you are walking with the Lord. The world will see the spiritual fruit that is being produced in you and will admire it. They may not realize where it is coming from but they will desire that in their lives as well. They may reject the Christ who is in you but they cannot deny the changes He makes in you. Just keep being faithful in following the Lord and these footsteps of following will lead to beautiful fruit in your life.

John 15:1-5 are the words of Jesus concerning fruitfulness. **"I am the true vine, and My Father is the vinedresser. Every branch in Me that does not bear fruit He takes away; and every *branch* that bears fruit He prunes, that it may bear more fruit. You are already clean because of the word which I have spoken to you. Abide in Me, and I in you. As the branch cannot bear fruit of itself, unless it abides in the vine, neither can you, unless you abide in Me. I am the vine, you *are* the branches. He who abides in Me, and I in him, bears much fruit; for without Me you can do nothing."** Note that walking in fruitfulness does not take a lot of effort. It only means that you abide in Christ Jesus and let the Holy Spirit work in you to produce the fruitfulness that God wants you to walk in. He does it all and we get to be what He wants us to be and do as He wants us to do.

Chapter Seven   Footsteps of Fury and Fighting

The Lord God is a loving and merciful God.   We know this because all through Scripture God is portrayed as One who wants to forgive and fellowship with all mankind. Isaiah 55:6 says, **Seek the LORD while He may be found, Call upon Him while He is near.** Psalm 86:5 declares, **For You, Lord, are good, and ready to forgive, And abundant in mercy to all those who call upon You.**

Furthermore, God is not only called a loving God but He is love itself. 1 John 4:7 tells us, **Beloved, let us love one another, for love is of God; and everyone who loves is born of God and knows God.** 1 John 4:16 goes on to say, **And we have known and believed the love that God has for us. God is love, and he who abides in love abides in God, and God in him.**

With the emphasis on the loving, forgiving, merciful and gracious character of God we sometimes forget that God is also perfectly holy, righteous and just. Exodus 15:11 states, **" Who is like You, O LORD, among the gods?**

Who is like You, glorious in holiness, Fearful in praises, doing wonders?"

Isaiah 45:21 are the words of God: **Tell and bring forth your case; Yes, let them take counsel together. Who has declared this from ancient time? Who has told it from that time? Have not I, the LORD? And there is no other God besides Me, A just God and a Savior; There is none besides Me.** Psalms 7:9 goes on to say, **Oh, let the wickedness of the wicked come to an end, But establish the just; For the righteous God tests the hearts and minds.**

The fact that God is both loving and holy in all perfection created a problem for mankind who, by himself, is not as holy and loving as God is. In order to live in fellowship with God we had to be clean from all sin and walk in righteousness. None of us could measure up and had the sentence of death in us; both physical and spiritual death. That is why Jesus came and paid the price for our sins by the sacrifice of Himself on the cross so that He died and shed His blood in our place so that by accepting Jesus as

Saviour and Lord, believing that He died and rose again for us, we could be saved and have His Spirit live within us. John, the disciple of Jesus wrote in John 1:14, **And the Word became flesh and dwelt among us, and we beheld His glory, the glory as of the only begotten of the Father, full of grace and truth.** Truth revealed our wickedness and the ultimate end of death for us. Grace brought God's favour to us through our lord Jesus Christ. Psalm 85:10 describes it this way: **Mercy and truth have met together; Righteousness and peace have kissed.**

Because God is holy and requires holiness in mankind, He cannot endure wickedness but must fight against all evil. Therefore He sometimes walks in paths of fury and fighting while all the time loving and desiring all to repent and come to forgiveness and receive His love. His nature demands it and so, while reaching out with love to all mankind, He must eventually punish all wickedness in those who do not repent and turn to His love and mercy.

God can get very angry. Psalm 76:7 declares, **You, Yourself, *are* to be feared; And who may stand in Your**

presence When once You are angry? Judges 2:20 tells us of a time when God became angry with His own people, Israel. **Then the anger of the LORD was hot against Israel; and He said, "Because this nation has transgressed My covenant which I commanded their fathers, and has not heeded My voice.**

Thank God that He is so merciful that He does not pour out His wrath until He has no other choice. Psalm 78:38 & 39 shows this aspect of God's character. **But He, being full of compassion, forgave their iniquity, And did not destroy them. Yes, many a time He turned His anger away, And did not stir up all His wrath; For He remembered that they were but flesh, A breath that passes away and does not come again.**

God's footsteps of anger come first before His footsteps of fighting. Isaiah 27:4 is an interesting verse: **Fury is not in Me. Who would set briers and thorns Against Me in battle? I would go through them, I would burn them together.** The background of this verse is the care that God gives for His people described as a vineyard.

As He cares for His people He is not walking in fury and considers the efforts of those who oppose Him to be futile. However, Psalm 7:11 states, **God is a just judge, And God is angry with the wicked every day.**

God called out to His people, Israel, to serve Him and prosper in His love and mercy but goes on to say in Leviticus 26:27 & 28**, 'And after all this, if you do not obey Me, but walk contrary to Me, then I also will walk contrary to you in fury; and I, even I, will chastise you seven times for your sins.'** Note that it was not that God did not try to forgive them and give them a good life. If the people stubbornly refused to follow God their Creator but to go astray and to do wrong, the Lord God had no choice but to come against them in fury. Even then, he would punish His people seven times (seven times being the sign of perfection) but would not seek to destroy them. Remember that God has to deal with deliberate sin in the lives of His people as well as in the ungodly.

David warns us to love the Son of God, Jesus, with our whole heart in the face of His fury in Psalm 2:12: **Kiss**

the Son, lest He be angry, And you perish in the way, When His wrath is kindled but a little. Blessed are all those who put their trust in Him. God has a right to expect us to love and honour Him, especially in the light of all that He has done for us. God only moves from fury to fighting as the time is right

Isaiah 63:3 shows the transition from fury to anger: **I have trodden the winepress alone, and from the peoples no one was with Me. For I have trodden them in My anger, and trampled them in My fury; their blood is sprinkled upon My garments, and I have stained all My robes**. These are footsteps of judgment from God for deliberate disobedience to Him and rejection of His love. These are the footsteps of God directed toward unrepentant, rebellious wickedness. These are the footsteps directed toward all who will not repent and turn to God in humility.

In the end times God will come with footsteps of fury and fighting against the nations who rebel against Him even as He cares for His people who have turned to Him. This is described in Isaiah 66:13-16: **As one whom his mother comforts, So I will comfort you; And you shall be comforted in Jerusalem." When you see** *this,* **your heart shall rejoice, And your bones shall flourish like grass; The hand of the LORD shall be known to His servants, And** *His* **indignation to His enemies. For behold, the LORD will come with fire And with His chariots, like a whirlwind, To render His anger with fury, And His rebuke with flames of fire. For by fire and by His sword The LORD will judge all flesh; And the slain of the LORD shall be many.** These are the end times footsteps of fighting with fury. Note the word "indignation" - an indication that God is finally fed up with the insults of mankind toward His abundant love and grace that they refuse to accept.

We walk in footsteps of God's fury and fighting in a different battle before we come to the end times. We can be filled with fury at times. Psalm 4:4 says, **Be angry, and do not sin. Meditate within your heart on your bed, and be still. Selah** . Ephesians 4:26 adds, **"Be angry, and do not sin": do not let the sun go down on your wrath.** Some

Christians use these verses to justify a bad temper. However, we are cautioned not to have unrighteous fury. Ecclesiastes 7:9 warns us, **Do not hasten in your spirit to be angry, For anger rests in the bosom of fools**. Also, remember Jonah in Jonah 4:1 & 4: **But it displeased Jonah exceedingly, and he became angry...Then the LORD said, "Is it right for you to be angry?"**

Proverbs 19:19 warns about uncontrolled wrath. *A man of* **great wrath will suffer punishment; For if you rescue** *him,* **you will have to do it again.** Jesus further warned about unjust fury in Matthew 5:22. **But I say to you that whoever is angry with his brother without a cause shall be in danger of the judgment. And whoever says to his brother, 'Raca!' shall be in danger of the council. But whoever says, 'You fool!' shall be in danger of hell fire** (Raca means empty one or worthless one). Calling someone empty-headed or a fool is usually done in anger and cannot be justified in our lives. It is wrong.

It is important to be angry at the right things. Selfish anger is wrong and needs repentance on our part.

Acceptable anger is aimed at that which is wrong: sin, injustice, abuse, ungodliness, wrongdoing, unloving speech and actions (this includes things that may be morally and ethically right but are not done in love). Remember Ephesians 4:14 & 15: **that we should no longer be children, tossed to and fro and carried about with every wind of doctrine, by the trickery of men, in the cunning craftiness of deceitful plotting, but, speaking the truth in love, may grow up in all things into Him who is the head --- Christ.** There is a lot of wickedness in the world against which we should be angry. Our anger should be aimed at the wrong, not at the individual who needs the love of Christ in his or her life desperately.

Our fight is spiritual. 2 Corinthians 10:3-5 explains, **For though we walk in the flesh, we do not war according to the flesh. For the weapons of our warfare *are* not carnal but mighty in God for pulling down strongholds, casting down arguments and every high thing that exalts itself against the knowledge of God, bringing every thought into captivity to the obedience**

of Christ. We are in a spiritual warfare that consists of many battles. Victory starts with an understanding that people are not our enemies but spiritual wickedness, Satan, the hosts of darkness and so on. Ephesians 6:12 says, **For we do not wrestle against flesh and blood, but against principalities, against powers, against the rulers of the darkness of this age, against spiritual hosts of wickedness in the heavenly places.** Therefore the footsteps of fury and fighting are not in the physical realm nor accomplished with physical means but spiritual.

Our weapons are **mighty in God for pulling down strongholds** (2 Corinthians 10:4) . Our spiritual weapons work by **casting down arguments and every high thing that exalts itself against the knowledge of God, bringing every thought into captivity to the obedience of Christ** (2 Corinthians 10:5).

This warfare works in the mind, in our thoughts. As God is given first place in our minds, He brings powerful truth against the arguments of the unspiritual and all that resists the knowledge of God. That is why it is so important to bring every thought into the captivity of obedience to Christ. Whenever we think of anything, we need to ask ourselves, "What does Jesus want?" and "How would Jesus think about this?"

Walking in footsteps of fury and fighting in this spiritual battle requires that we use our spiritual weapons. Ephesians 6:10 & 11 encourage us, **Finally, my brethren, be strong in the Lord and in the power of His might. Put on the whole armor of God, that you may be able to stand against the wiles of the devil.** Ephesians 6:14-17 identifies our spiritual weapons: **Stand therefore, having girded your waist with truth, having put on the breastplate of righteousness, and having shod your feet with the preparation of the gospel of peace; above all, taking the shield of faith with which you will be able to quench all the fiery darts of the wicked one. And take the helmet of salvation, and the sword of the Spirit, which is the word of God;** We must walk uprightly in the righteousness of Christ.

Protect your head with the helmet of salvation which is through Christ Jesus. Romans 10:10 says, **For with the heart one believes unto righteousness, and with the mouth confession is made unto salvation.** 2 Corinthians 1:30 says, **But of Him you are in Christ Jesus, who became for us wisdom from God --- and righteousness and sanctification and redemption ---** which is your helmet and breastplate protecting your head and body.

Walk in the preparation of the gospel of peace. 1 Peter 3:15 tells us, **But sanctify the Lord God in your hearts, and always be ready to give a defense to everyone who asks you a reason for the hope that is in you, with meekness and fear;**

Shield yourself with faith. Romans 10:17 informs us, **So then faith comes by hearing, and hearing by the word of God.** Faith initially is a gift from God. Romans 12:3 bears this out: **For I say, through the grace given to me, to everyone who is among you, not to think of himself more highly than he ought to think, but to think soberly, as God has dealt to each one a measure of faith.** Then we grow our faith by dwelling on the Word of God and letting it speak to us. Romans 10:17 explains, **So then faith comes by hearing, and hearing by the word of God.**

Attack the enemy with the Scriptures, not your own wisdom. Ephesians 10:11b tells us to use **the sword of the Spirit, which is the word of God.** Jesus used the Word of God in the wilderness temptation that He went through (Matthew 4; Mark 1). Ephesians 10:18 goes on to include prayer with our spiritual weapon and tells us how to do battle: **praying always with all prayer and supplication in the Spirit, being watchful to this end with all perseverance and supplication for all the saints.**

My daughter, Cindy, phoned me one day to tell me of a dream that she had about the forces of darkness fighting with the forces of light. The demons and angels were fighting but she saw no weapons in their hands. Although the Scripture is clear that our sword is the Word of God, the sword of the Holy Spirit, we are told in Ephesians 6:12, **For we do not wrestle against flesh and blood, but against principalities, against powers, against the rulers of the**

darkness of this age, against spiritual hosts of wickedness in the heavenly places. It does not mention any weapons in this verse. It would indicate that at times we are to resist the enemy as he attacks us with testing or temptation and wrestle against his efforts in the mental and spiritual realm. Resist the enemy in the name of Jesus and by the power of the blood of Jesus that was shed for you. James 4:7 tells us, **Therefore submit to God. Resist the devil and he will flee from you.**

It is interesting that 1 Thessalonians 5:8 says, **But let us who are of the day be sober, putting on the breastplate of faith and love, and *as* a helmet the hope of salvation.** Here the breastplate is identified as faith and love and the helmet as the hope of salvation and not just salvation. Righteousness is the fabric of God's work in the breastplate and faith and love are the fabrics that are woven into the breastplate by God's power in us. All of these things are protections for the believer.

If you have not made Jesus Christ your Saviour you cannot successfully follow in the footsteps of fury and fighting. If you are not maintaining a regular prayer life and study in the Word of God you will falter in these footsteps for these footsteps are not for the faint of heart.

Above all else, depend on God to help you because you can do nothing without Him. Jesus said in John 15:5,**"I am the vine, you are the branches. He who abides in Me, and I in him, bears much fruit; for without Me you can do nothing."**

Those who know Jesus as Saviour and Lord, if they are already in heaven, will return with Him in victorious footsteps of fury and fighting to establish righteousness on the earth and the rule of Christ on all. This is not our battle now but those who have died in Christ will be coming back with Him to execute the fury of God in fighting against the wicked of the earth at that day. Jude 1:14 &15 says, **Now Enoch, the seventh from Adam, prophesied about these men also, saying, "Behold, the Lord comes with ten thousands of His saints, to execute judgment on all, to convict all who are ungodly among them of all their ungodly deeds which they have committed in an**

ungodly way, and of all the harsh things which ungodly sinners have spoken against Him."

There is an old song that says "It's a battlefield, brother, not a recreation field. It's a fight and not a game. Run if you want to. Run if you will, but I came here to stay". I trust that with Joshua in Joshua 24:15 we will all say, **But as for me and my house, we will serve the LORD."** Let us determine that we will stand strong for the Lord regardless of what battle the enemy may send our way and continue walking in His footsteps. We will be victorious as we follow in God's footsteps of fury and fighting.

Chapter Eight   Footsteps of Forever Presence

Loneliness is painful. Experts in psychology tell us that loneliness produces one of the most painful emotions that a person can experience. Funk And Wagnalls Dictionary identifies loneliness as the condition a person might have of being "1. Unfrequented by human beings; deserted; desolate. 2. Sad from lack of companionship or sympathy; lonesome." The pain of loneliness is often a feeling that no-one knows or cares or understands. It is a feeling of being all alone. The gospel song "Where No-one Stands Alone" by Mosie Lister declares But "I don't know a thing In this whole wide world That's worse than being alone".

People can be lonely because no-one is around. People stranded in an isolated place sometimes break down mentally because of the lack of human contact. However, people can face loneliness in the midst of a crowd where there are many around simply because no-one else understands or appears to do so. That is one of the terrible dangers of bullying or mocking; it leads to low self esteem and a sense of loneliness and fear. Life can seem hopeless. There seems to be nowhere to turn for help.

Loneliness has caused people to do terrible things. Some have committed suicide. Some have turned in anger towards others, sometimes with violence and even murder. Some have retreated into a world separate from reality, which is termed "insanity". Some have retreated physically from the rest of society to live in isolation.

God promises in His Word that we never need to be lonely because He leads us with His forever presence. Isaiah 43:1-3 was God's promise to His people Israel: **But now, thus says the LORD, who created you, O Jacob, And He who formed you, O Israel: " Fear not, for I have redeemed you; I have called you by your name; You are Mine. When you pass through the waters, I will be with you; And through the rivers, they shall not overflow you. When you walk through the fire, you shall not be burned, Nor shall the flame scorch you. For I am the LORD your God, The Holy One of Israel, your Savior; I**

gave Egypt for your ransom, Ethiopia and Seba in your place. No matter where the Lord led Israel, He would be with them. Whether they were going through water, rivers, fire and flame God promised that they were not alone. He would be with His people.

This promise is also to all who are God's people through the sacrifice of Jesus on the cross; Galatians 3:13 & 14 says, **Christ has redeemed us from the curse of the law, having become a curse for us (for it is written, *"Cursed is everyone who hangs on a tree"*), that the blessing of Abraham might come upon the Gentiles in Christ Jesus, that we might receive the promise of the Spirit through faith.** The Abrahamic blessing of God's presence can be ours today.

Psalm 23:1-4 is a portion of Scripture that many can quote: **The LORD is my shepherd; I shall not want. He makes me to lie down in green pastures; he leads me beside the still waters. He restores my soul; he leads me in the paths of righteousness for His name's sake. Yea, though I walk through the valley of the shadow of**

death, I will fear no evil; for You are with me; your rod and Your staff, they comfort me. These are the footsteps of God's forever presence. Note that in this psalm God's footsteps lead us if we are willing to be led.

We walk in plenty so there is no lack. "**I shall not want**" means that I want for nothing. All my needs are met. By the way, it does not say, "All my desires are met" but rather, it is all my wants that are met. Psalms 37:4 & 5 explains it more clearly. **Delight yourself also in the LORD, And He shall give you the desires of your heart. Commit your way to the LORD, Trust also in Him, And He shall bring it to pass.** In the Hebrew text there is no word "also" in verse 4. The literal Hebrew rendering of these verses from the Interlinear Bible by Hendrickson is "**And delight yourself in Jehovah; that He may give you the desires of your heart. Roll on Jehovah your way; and trust in Him, and He will work.**" In other words, because your delight is in the Lord, His desires become your desires. You roll the desires of having your own way on to the Lord so that your own selfish desires vanish as you trust in Him to do what is best and so He then works out what is best for you.

The Lord leads us in green pastures where there is good nourishment for His sheep. Other people, organizations and philosophies will try to lead us otherwise but God leads us into what is good. We need to feed on His Word just as the sheep feed on good grass. Also, God sometimes makes us lie down in these pastures. We do not always have to be feeding on the Word although this is necessary for our spiritual health. Sometimes God just wants us to rest in His Word and be refreshed in His presence. Some people lie down and "soak in God's presence". This can be beneficial on many fronts. First of all, it causes us to slow down our hectic pace and stop what we are stressed over. It also causes us to focus on the Lord instead of ourselves or other things. It is restful and we experience the love and peace of God as He reaches out to us with His presence.

God leads His own beside still waters so there is refreshment. My dad used to raise sheep. They liked calmer waters that were flowing gently by. Rushing water scared the sheep but calm waters were more pleasing to the sheep. The waters needed to be flowing gently, though, or the sheep would muddy up their drinking water with their feet. (Actually, God's comparison of His people to sheep is not all that complimentary. We do foolish things like sheep too. My daughter says that sheep are dumb and if they fall on their backs they don't know to roll over.) Note that God's way is the way of refreshment and inner peace for His children. The water is most often symbolic of the Holy Spirit in Scripture. As we drink of the living water that Jesus gives us the Hoy Spirit within us refreshes us so that this living water flows out of us to others. Jesus spoke of this in John 7:38. **"He who believes in Me, as the Scripture has said, out of his heart** (literally, belly or innermost being) **will flow rivers of living water."** We need to trust the Great Shepherd of the sheep to lead us in the refreshing waters of God. All of this leads to the restoration of the soul. It is only the Lord God who can restore our souls. As the Shepherd of the sheep He does that for us. When we feel discouraged, down in spirit, sick, hurting or just down, as we turn to Him and let Him lead, we are restored inside of us, within our souls.

The forever footsteps of God lead us in paths of rightness or righteousness. Note that it is for His name's sake. He is honoured when we follow Him in paths of righteousness. When the world sees the likeness of God in us, they recognize the love and greatness of our God and He is glorified in us. The glory of the presence of God radiates to the world around us if we are walking in those footsteps that He is leading us in.

We can never walk in paths of righteousness unless we walk in His forever presence. He will invite us to walk in the right path but we must stay in His presence. The story of the prodigal son in Luke 15:11-32 illustrates this clearly. We reject His presence when we choose to do wrong contrary to God and His nature. We also reject His presence when we choose to do our own thing our own way whether it is done for self glory or even if we think we are doing it for His glory. We must not only do things for God but we must do it His way and according to His love and guidance.

Colossians 3:17 tells us, **And whatever you do in word or deed, do all in the name of the Lord Jesus, giving thanks to God the Father through Him**. Doing all in the name of the Lord means to do all according to all that the name of Jesus represents and requires that it be done in His way and for His glory. When a ruler asked Jesus the way to receive eternal life, Luke 10:27 says, **So he answered and said, "'You shall love the LORD your God with all your heart, with all your soul, with all your strength, and with all your mind,' and 'your neighbour as yourself.' "**In pleasing God we also must be endeavouring to show love to our neighbours as well.

Walking in the forever presence of God means comfort through the valley of the shadow of death. Much has been written by Christian commentators about the valley of the shadow of death. However, only in Psalm 23 is the valley of the shadow of death mentioned in Scripture. However, the shadow of death is mentioned many times. In Job 10:21, Job called Sheol or the grave, ``**the land of darkness and the shadow of death.**`` When John the

Baptist was a baby, his father, Zacharias, prophesied of him in Luke 1:76-79: **" And you, child, will be called the prophet of the Highest; For you will go before the face of the Lord to prepare His ways, To give knowledge of salvation to His people By the remission of their sins, Through the tender mercy of our God, With which the Dayspring from on high has visited us; To give light to those who sit in darkness and the shadow of death, To guide our feet into the way of peace."** John presented the Dayspring, Jesus of Nazareth, to a world lost in spiritual darkness and heading to hell, the culmination of spiritual death. The shadow of death, in this case, referred to those who face death spiritually. That refers to all of us who spiritually are initially without Christ Jesus in our lives. It also refers to all who face death physically.

An interesting observation is that you cannot see a shadow unless there is a substantially bright light. The shadow is caused by something coming between you and the light. We know from many Scriptures that Jesus says that He is the light and we, also who have the Holy Spirit in us, are the light of the world. When death comes between the light of God's presence we see the shadow of death. We may be facing threatening danger, the death of a loved one or ones around us that we don't even know or death coming for us personally. Whatever the purpose of the approach of death, remember the light of God is very near so we see the shadow of death.

We do not need to fear death because even when it looks us in the face, God is with us. We need only put our trust in Jesus Christ and walk with the Lord. Psalm 116:15 tells us, **Precious in the sight of the LORD Is the death of His saints.**

Through all things God`s comforting presence is there. God comforts those who walk with Him. That implies that there are difficult times in life that cause us to need comforting. We have all found this to be true. As we walk in God`s forever presence, He is there to comfort us. In Hebrews 13:5 God has promised us, **Let your conduct be without covetousness; be content with such things as you have. For He Himself has said, "I will never leave**

you nor forsake you." The Holy Spirit lives in every believer so God is ever in us and with us. 1 Corinthians 6:19 says, **Or do you not know that your body is the temple of the Holy Spirit *who is* in you, whom you have from God, and you are not your own?** Ephesians 4:4-6 go on to say, **There is one body and one Spirit, just as you were called in one hope of your calling; one Lord, one faith, one baptism; one God and Father of all, who is above all, and through all, and in you all.** 2 Corinthians 13:5 says, **Examine yourselves as to whether you are in the faith. Test yourselves. Do you not know yourselves, that Jesus Christ is in you? --- unless indeed you are disqualified.** God the Father, the Holy Spirit and Christ Jesus dwells in the believer and so God is ever present to comfort and direct the believer if we only choose to walk in His steps.

Matthew 28:18-20 tell us, **And Jesus came and spoke to them, saying, "All authority has been given to Me in heaven and on earth. Go therefore and make disciples of all the nations, baptizing them in the name**

of the Father and of the Son and of the Holy Spirit, teaching them to observe all things that I have commanded you; and lo, I am with you always, *even* to the end of the age." Amen. This is often called the Great Commission. Here Jesus gives the job description for the church: Go, make disciples everywhere, baptize them in the name of the Father, Son and Holy Spirit and teach them to do all that Jesus had taught. Besides this, Jesus gives us two assurances: First, all authority in heaven and earth has been given to Him so that we can successfully minister in His name with authority. Secondly, Jesus wanted us to know that He is with us at all times. We need not feel like orphans. His presence is always with us forever.

1 John 4:4 encourages us with the words of the Lord's forever presence, speaking of false prophets who would come: **You are of God, little children, and have overcome them, because He who is in you is greater than he who is in the world.** We overcome because He who is greater than all is in us and gives us His forever

presence. We need never feel as if we are alone. Walk confidently in the forever footsteps of God.

Chapter Nine   Footsteps of Fearlessness

This world can be a very frightening world. Dangers abound both in the world of nature and from people. The apostle Paul tells how he faced many fearful situations in his life. Defending his apostleship, Paul begins to compare himself with the other apostles and then shares his hardships in 2 Corinthians 11:23-28: **Are they ministers of Christ? --- I speak as a fool --- I *am* more: in labors more abundant, in stripes above measure, in prisons more frequently, in deaths often. From the Jews five times I received forty *stripes* minus one. Three times I was beaten with rods; once I was stoned; three times I was shipwrecked; a night and a day I have been in the deep;**

in journeys often, *in* perils of waters, *in* perils of robbers, *in* perils of *my own* countrymen, *in* perils of the Gentiles, *in* perils in the city, *in* perils in the wilderness, *in* perils in the sea, *in* perils among false brethren; in weariness and toil, in sleeplessness often, in hunger and thirst, in fastings often, in cold and

nakedness --- besides the other things, what comes upon me daily: my deep concern for all the churches. Talk about frightening situations! Paul certainly knew all about that.

Think about the three Hebrew slaves of King Nebuchadnezzar, king of Babylon whom we looked at earlier. Because they refused to bow down and worship the king's golden idol, he had them thrown into a fiery furnace, (probably a metal smelting furnace), and it was heated seven times hotter than usual. Daniel 3:19-23 tells us, **Then Nebuchadnezzar was full of fury, and the expression on his face changed toward Shadrach, Meshach, and Abed-Nego. He spoke and commanded that they heat the furnace seven times more than it was usually heated. And he commanded certain mighty men of valor who *were* in his army to bind Shadrach, Meshach, and Abed-Nego, *and* cast *them* into the burning fiery furnace. Then these men were bound in their coats, their trousers, their turbans, and their *other* garments, and were cast into the midst of the burning fiery** furnace. **Therefore, because the king's command was urgent, and the furnace exceedingly hot, the flame of the fire killed those men who took up Shadrach, Meshach, and Abed-Nego. And these three men, Shadrach, Meshach, and Abed-Nego, fell down bound into the midst of the burning fiery furnace.** Frightening indeed! However, God delivered them from death and even from being burned. Daniel 3:24-27 go on to say, **Then King Nebuchadnezzar was astonished; and he rose in haste *and* spoke, saying to his counselors, "Did we not cast three men bound into the midst of the fire?" They answered and said to the king, "True, O king." "Look!" he answered, "I see four men loose, walking in the midst of the fire; and they are not hurt, and the form of the fourth is like the Son of God." Then Nebuchadnezzar went near the mouth of the burning fiery furnace *and* spoke, saying, "Shadrach, Meshach, and Abed-Nego, servants of the Most High God, come out, and come *here.*" Then Shadrach, Meshach, and Abed-Nego came from the midst of the fire. And the**

satraps, administrators, governors, and the king's counselors gathered together, and they saw these men on whose bodies the fire had no power; the hair of their head was not singed nor were their garments affected, and the smell of fire was not on them. A miracle to be sure but certainly it was a frightening ordeal for those three young Hebrew men.

There is a song about the Three Hebrew teenagers thrown into the fiery furnace written by Walt Mills called, "He's Still In The Fire". Part of it goes like this: "Then I said, 'Mama, wait a minute, there's one thing that I must know, If three went in and three came out, then where'd that fourth man go?" And I never will forget it, as Mama danced across the floor, These are the words I heard her say as she shouted through the door. Son, He's still in the fire and He's walking in the flame, And He'll be there to help you when you call in Jesus' name, And He can still deliver by His almighty power. While here below it's good to know He's still in the fire." A scary experience it was for sure but the Lord goes with us in steps of fearlessness whatever we face, even when we feel we are going through the fire.

God's promise to Israel that can be assurance to all of God's people is found in Isaiah 43:1-3: **But now, thus says the LORD, who created you, O Jacob, And He who formed you, O Israel: " Fear not, for I have redeemed you; I have called *you* by your name; You *are* Mine. When you pass through the waters, I *will be* with you; And through the rivers, they shall not overflow you. When you walk through the fire, you shall not be burned, Nor shall the flame scorch you. For I *am* the LORD your God, The Holy One of Israel, your Savior...** The emphasis is on the word "**through**" and "**I will be with you**". We need not fear because the Lord goes with us and, though we may have to go through the water, rivers, fire and flame, we will not be destroyed for God goes with us.

There are many other frightening situations all through Scripture. We remember the slavery of the Israelites in Egypt. The struggles of the Israelites in their journey to the promised land is epic. Who can forget about

Daniel' visit to the lions' den or Elijah's encounters with the wicked queen Jezebel and her sinful husband, Ahab?

Even when Jesus was with the disciples were there frightening incidents. One such event happened when Jesus sent the disciple out on the Sea of Galilee while He stayed back on shore. It was stormy and the waves were quite high. Then we read in Matthew 14:25-29, **Now in the fourth watch of the night Jesus went to them, walking on the sea. And when the disciples saw Him walking on the sea, they were troubled, saying, "It is a ghost!" And they cried out for fear. But immediately Jesus spoke to them, saying, "Be of good cheer! It is I; do not be afraid." And Peter answered Him and said, "Lord, if it is You, command me to come to You on the water." So He said, "Come." And when Peter had come down out of the boat, he walked on the water to go to Jesus.**

The disciples were anxious because of the dangers of being out on the lake in a storm. Most of them had been fishermen on this lake and knew what the dangers were. Then they saw what they thought was a ghost walking on the water toward them. I can only imagine how scared I might have been too.

Calling out to the Lord, they realized that this water walker was, in fact, Jesus, their Lord and Saviour. The lesson we learn from this is that in the midst of the storm God walks to us. He's always there keeping watch over us in the midst of our storms.

These are the steps of fearlessness. Note Jesus' words to His disciples, **"Be of good cheer! It is I; do not be afraid."** In other words, "Be happy. I'm here so there's no need to have any fear." In a stormy lake, in a small boat, that would sound ridiculous except for the fact that the words were coming from the Lord Jesus.

In the middle of our storms He invites us to take the step of faith and get out of the boat and walk on top of the stormy water by keeping our eyes on Him and not on the storm. Some people find fault with Peter because he took his eyes off Jesus, looked at the circumstances around him (the wild waves) and started to sink. However, I admire him because he was the only one willing to get out of the boat and try to walk toward Jesus. As with Peter, if we get out in the storm to walk with Jesus and begin to falter, Jesus will reach out and rescue us. He never asks us to go where He will not go with us and be our support and strength.

God walks in pathways of fearlessness because He is greater than, and over, all creation. John 10:29 says, **My Father, who has given them to Me, is greater than all;** and then, referring to our security in Him continues with, **and no one is able to snatch them out of My Father's hand.** Therefore, God walks without fear and nothing can happen to us that does not go through His hands first. God is never surprised by anything that comes our way. Things that we view as terrible and horrific that we go through may be bad but God allows it to purify and mature us in Him. Zechariah 13:9 is the Lord talking: **"I will bring the one-third through the fire, Will refine them as silver is refined, And test them as gold is tested. They will call on My name, And I will answer them. I will say, 'This is My people'; And each one will say, 'The LORD is my God.' "** From God's point of view, which is the eternal view, the badness we go through is just temporary and is nothing compared to the glory that He has for us. Job recognized this when he said in Job 23:10, **But He knows the way that I take; When He has tested me, I shall come forth as gold**.

The apostle John reminds us of God in 1 John 4:18-19, **There is no fear in love; but perfect love casts out fear, because fear involves torment. But he who fears has not been made perfect in love. We love Him because He first loved us**. While we need to have an awesome respect for who God is, referred to in Scripture as the fear of God, we need not be scared because of the way God leads us. The fact that God is awesome in His greatness is our assurance that, because He loves us perfectly, we do not need to walk in the path of fear. We have the assurance in 1 John 4:16, **And we have known and believed the love that God has for us. God is love, and he who abides in love abides in God, and God in him.**

Since God is almighty and is perfect love (1 John 4:8), we can walk with Him in the footsteps of fearlessness. Come what may, God is with us. Come what may, God is on our side so that we can say with the apostle Paul in Romans 8:35-37, **Who shall separate us from the love of Christ?** ***Shall*** **tribulation, or distress, or persecution, or famine, or nakedness, or peril, or sword? As it is written: " For Your sake we are killed all day long; We are accounted as sheep for the slaughter." Yet in all these things we are more than conquerors through Him who loved us.** We can walk in footsteps of fearlessness because God is walking without fear with us.

God's footsteps, in relation to us do not end here on this earth. God's footsteps go heavenward and so we can follow these footsteps as well, either at death or when Jesus Christ returns for His own. We have a future glory in eternity.

The word, "glory" is an interesting study in itself. Sufficient for now is the understanding that the manifestation of visible brightness in relation to God, as well as a dark cloud of His presence, our praises and exaltation of God are all referred to as glory when referring to the Lord. When referring to mankind, glory can mean blessings, exaltation or manifestations of God's presence in us such as, what some people call, the warm of His presence .

The glory we receive from God's blessings and victories in our lives on this earth cause us to sing praises to God as we give thanks to Him forever. Psalm 30:11 & 12 displays the psalmist's rejoicing with, **You have turned for me my mourning into dancing; You have put off my sackcloth and clothed me with gladness, To the end that *my* glory**

may sing praise to You and not be silent. O LORD my God, I will give thanks to You forever.

We can walk in the glory presence of God as He manifests His presence in our midst according to His will and purposes. Some have witnessed the shekinah glory of God as a thick cloud of God's presence in meetings. I personally attended a meeting where we were just getting started when a strong smell of smoke, something like the smell of incense was being smelled by many. The church's head usher thought that someone was smoking marijuana outside. Someone else thought it was from burning leaves as it was autumn. I went all through the building looking for any smoke or source of fire and there was nothing. Two ushers went outside and there was no smoke from anything outside. When we returned to the main meeting room one of the ushers went up to the front where the visiting evangelist was sitting and said that everything was fine. The evangelist went up on the platform, stopped the worship team in the middle of leading the singing and asked how many people had smelled smoke. I guess that about two thirds to three quarters of the congregation raised their hands. He declared, "I believe that the smell of smoke is a manifestation of God's presence." The instant that he said that, the smell of smoke turned into a smell like perfume something like lily of the valley. Many people witnessed that and people began to praise God for His greatness and His favour on us. One lady, with tears in her eyes, declared, "That has to be God."

The people of Israel in their desert wanderings also experienced much of the same. Exodus 24:17 tells us of one time that the Israelites saw the manifested glory of God: **The sight of the glory of the LORD was like a consuming fire on the top of the mountain in the eyes of the children of Israel.** Exodus 20:21 also tells us of the manifested glory of God on Mount Sinai: **So the people stood afar off, but Moses drew near the thick darkness where God was.**

That God walks in glory is evident from the fulfillment of Moses' interaction with God in Exodus 33:12-18. **Then Moses said to the LORD, "See, You say to me, 'Bring up** this people.' But You have not let me know whom You will send with me. Yet You have said, 'I know you by name, and you have also found grace in My sight.' Now therefore, I pray, if I have found grace in Your sight, show me now Your way, that I may know You and that I may find grace in Your sight. And consider that this nation is Your people." And He said, "My Presence will go with you, and I will give you rest." Then he said to Him, "If Your Presence does not go with us, do not bring us up from here. For how then will it be known that Your people and I have found grace in Your sight, except You go with us? So we shall be separate, Your people and I, from all the people who are upon the face of the earth." So the LORD said to Moses, "I will also do this thing that you have spoken; for you have found grace in My sight, and I know you by name." And he said, "Please, show me Your glory."

The request to see God's glory was bold. Moses had already seen the manifestation of God's glory on Mount Sinai in the cloud and the fire. This was different. This was extremely bold. No-one in a physical body could look at God and live because the power and majesty of His being would take away the life of that person. Yet, because God was showing special favour to Moses by promising that His actual Presence would go with him, Moses wanted to see His Presence in a manifested form, not just sense Him or hear from Him.

Amazingly, God agreed to reveal Himself bodily to Moses. Exodus 33:19-23 gives us this encounter. **Then He said, "I will make all My goodness pass before you, and I will proclaim the name of the LORD before you. I will be gracious to whom I will be gracious, and I will have compassion on whom I will have compassion." But He said, "You cannot see My face; for no man shall see Me, and live." And the LORD said, "Here is a place by Me, and you shall stand on the rock. So it shall be, while My glory passes by, that I will put you in the cleft of the rock, and will cover you with My hand while I pass by. Then I will take away My hand, and you shall see My back; but My face shall not be seen."**

So great was the effect on Moses that his face shone with the glory of God. Exodus 34:29,30 & 33 say, **Now it was so, when Moses came down from Mount Sinai (and the two tablets of the Testimony were in Moses' hand when he came down from the mountain), that Moses did not know that the skin of his face shone while he talked with Him. So when Aaron and all the children of Israel saw Moses, behold, the skin of his face shone, and they were afraid to come near him.. And when Moses had finished speaking with them, he put a veil on his face.**

God has always walked in footsteps of glory but He has seldom revealed them to mankind. However, that is going to change. We will, in the future, walk with Him in footsteps of glory. We see small glimpses of the glory of God now as His children but it will be fully manifested in heaven to His own.

In John 17:22-24, Jesus prayed the following to the heavenly Father. **"And the glory which You gave Me I have given them, that they may be one just as We are one: I in them, and You in Me; that they may be made perfect in one, and that the world may know that You**

have sent Me, and have loved them as You have loved Me. Father, I desire that they also whom You gave Me may be with Me where I am, that they may behold My glory which You have given Me; for You loved Me before the foundation of the world." The glory that Jesus has given His followers for now is very little compared to the glory of Jesus that will be seen in heaven.

2 Corinthians 3:18 tells us that we are being changed by one glory after another until we reach eternity. **But we all, with unveiled face, beholding as in a mirror the glory of the Lord, are being transformed into the same image from glory to glory, just as by the Spirit of the Lord.** The Spirit of the Lord works in us to cause us to walk more and more in the footsteps of glory on this earth.

The apostle Paul says of Jesus in Romans 5:2, **through whom also we have access by faith into this grace in which we stand, and rejoice in hope of the glory of God.** We have the hope of seeing the glory of God as we walk in future glory with the Lord.

The hope that we have of walking in footsteps of future

glory helps us to endure trials and difficulties in this life on earth. Romans 8:18 gives us this encouragement. **For I consider that the sufferings of this present time are not worthy to be compared with the glory which shall be revealed in us.** 2 Corinthians 4:17 confirms this thought: **For our light affliction, which is but for a moment, is working for us a far more exceeding and eternal weight of glory,**

1 Peter 4:12 & 13 are Peter's words of encouragement in **this matter: Beloved, do not think it strange concerning the fiery trial which is to try you, as though some strange thing happened to you; but rejoice to the extent that you partake of Christ's sufferings, that when His glory is revealed, you may also be glad with exceeding joy.** The old song, It Will Be Worth It All When We See Jesus rings loud and clear. It is our certain hope. We shall walk in glory with Jesus.

Paul prayed in Ephesians 1:18 **for the eyes of your understanding being enlightened; that you may know what is the hope of His calling, what are the riches of**

the glory of His inheritance in the saints. We need to understand that this glory has untold riches for us to discover. Colossians 1:27 gives us an inkling into what this glory will be. **To them God willed to make known what are the riches of the glory of this mystery among the Gentiles: which is Christ in you, the hope of glory.**

Christ will be in us in His revealed glory in eternity. 1 John 3:2 says, **Beloved, now we are children of God; and it has not yet been revealed what we shall be, but we know that when He is revealed, we shall be like Him, for we shall see Him as He is.**

When we get to eternity with God our steps will be in sync with His. We will walk in His footsteps forever enjoying His eternal presence in future glory.

Chapter Eleven   Final Thoughts

Psalm 25 is a prayer of David. Verse four says, **Show me Your ways, O LORD; Teach me Your paths.** Verse ten goes on to declare, **All the paths of the LORD *are* mercy and truth, To such as keep His covenant and His testimonies.** What encouragement this is to all who put their trust in the Lord Jesus.

Matthew 3:1-3 gives us a picture of Jesus' cousin, John: **In those days John the Baptist came preaching in the wilderness of Judea, and saying, "Repent, for the kingdom of heaven is at hand!" For this is he who was spoken of by the prophet Isaiah, saying: " The voice of one crying in the wilderness: ' Prepare the way of the LORD; Make His paths straight.' "** This is an interesting portion of Scripture. John was calling his people, the Jews, to make the Lord's path straight. What did this mean?

Obviously the meaning was not to fix the potholes in the highway as no-one knew which road Jesus would be walking on. The explanation is clearer when referring to the original declaration. Isaiah 40:3 is the portion of Scripture that is quoted by Matthew. It says, **The voice of one crying in the wilderness: " Prepare the way of the LORD; Make straight in the desert A highway for our God.** While people in those days were often required to fix up the road that a king would be travelling on to make the way straight and smooth, the meaning here is spiritual. The desert is a spiritual dearth or famine in the hearts of the people. They were dry and in need of the water of life that only Jesus could bring. They were to prepare the way of the Lord by preparing their hearts to receive Jesus, His forgiveness and His truth. If we are to walk in the footsteps of God we, too, must prepare our hearts to walk in His steps.

Hearts that are prepared to walk in God's footsteps are first of all, hearts of humility. Psalm 25:9 says, **The humble He guides in justice, And the humble He teaches His way.**

Proverbs 3:5-7 shows us the way to walk in God's footsteps. **Trust in the LORD with all your heart, And lean not on your own understanding; In all your ways**

acknowledge Him, And He shall direct your paths. Do not be wise in your own eyes; Fear the LORD and depart from evil. You are not to depend on your own knowledge or wisdom but to put your total trust in God and His wisdom. Total trust means total humility where your will is put aside and only what God wants and where He is leading matters. The Lord must be recognized in all of our decisions and directions that we take. After all, if we are to follow the footsteps of God, we have to forget about following our own paths and follow His instead.

When we follow in the steps of our Lord and Master we will follow in good steps that give us security for our way. Psalm 37:23, 24 & 31 tell us, **The steps of a *good* man are ordered by the LORD, And He delights in his way. Though he fall, he shall not be utterly cast down; For the LORD upholds *him with* His hand...The law of his God *is* in his heart; None of his steps shall slide.** This means that although we may trip and fall in our walk with God, He will always pick us up and not allow our feet to slip or slide off the path that is good for us. David's prayer request in Psalm 17:5 says, **"Uphold my steps in Your paths, That my footsteps may not slip"**, have a certain assurance of fulfillment because the Lord has promised He would keep our steps from slipping.

We must remember that it is God Himself who rescued us from the pit of sin and judgment and established our footsteps to follow his steps. Psalm 40:2 declares, **He also brought me up out of a horrible pit, Out of the miry clay, And set my feet upon a rock,** *And* **established my steps.** He who established our footsteps, when we accepted Jesus Christ as Saviour and Lord, will keep us and give us strength and direction to continue to walk in right paths as we follow His footsteps.

We need to be sensitive to God's leading in our lives. He often speaks to us by the Holy Spirit by means of His quiet voice inside us. He also speaks by His Spirit through the Word of God. After all, the Word of God was produced through men by the Holy Spirit (2 Peter 1:21 and 2 Timothy 3:16). Proverbs 4:11 & 12 assure us, **I have taught you in the way of wisdom; I have led you in right paths. When** you walk, your steps will not be hindered, And when you run, you will not stumble.

Although the path God ordains for each person to walk through life is different from all others, that path is chosen by God and He walks ahead of each one to prepare the way. David put it this way in Psalm 16:11, **You will show me the path of life; In Your presence is fullness of joy; At Your right hand are pleasures forevermore.** Psalm 139:3 says, **You comprehend my path and my lying down, And are acquainted with all my ways**.

Our responsibility is to know the Word of God and follow it for it will give light to the path on which we walk. Psalm 119:105 tells us, **Your word is a lamp to my feet And a light to my path.** God is faithful to show us His footsteps to walk in if we just take the time to listen to His Word. That is why Proverbs 4:26 warns us, **Ponder the path of your feet, And let all your ways be established.**

Proverbs 10:29 encourages us with the understanding that His footsteps lead in a way that gives strength to those who walk in it. **The way of the LORD is strength for the**

upright, But destruction will come to the workers of iniquity. God wants us to gain strength as His upright people, people who walk in His footsteps.

As you have already seen, the footsteps of God have many aspects. My breakdown is simply a human effort to show how great our God is and what following the Lord entails. Don't think of it as comprehensive or complete in any way. It has been an effort to cause us to appreciate our loving God more than ever before and to walk in confidence in His footsteps, knowing that His way is always the best.

I encourage you to make God's footsteps yours to follow and then one day you will walk with Him right into eternity and the glory of God that awaits all who follow in His footsteps.

49324248R00087

Made in the USA
Charleston, SC
23 November 2015